Valerian Gribayédoff

The French Invasion of Ireland in '98

Leaves of Unwritten History that Tell of an Heroic Endeavor and.....

THE FRENCH

INVASION OF IRELAND IN '98

LEAVES OF UNWRITTEN HISTORY

THAT TELL OF AN

HEROIC ENDEAVOR

AND A

LOST OPPORTUNITY

TO THROW OFF ENGLAND'S YOKE

BY

VALERIAN GRIBAYÉDOFF

WITH A MAP, AND NUMEROUS ILLUSTRATIONS BY
WELL-KNOWN ARTISTS

NEW YORK
CHARLES P. SOMERBY
28 LAFAYETTE PLACE

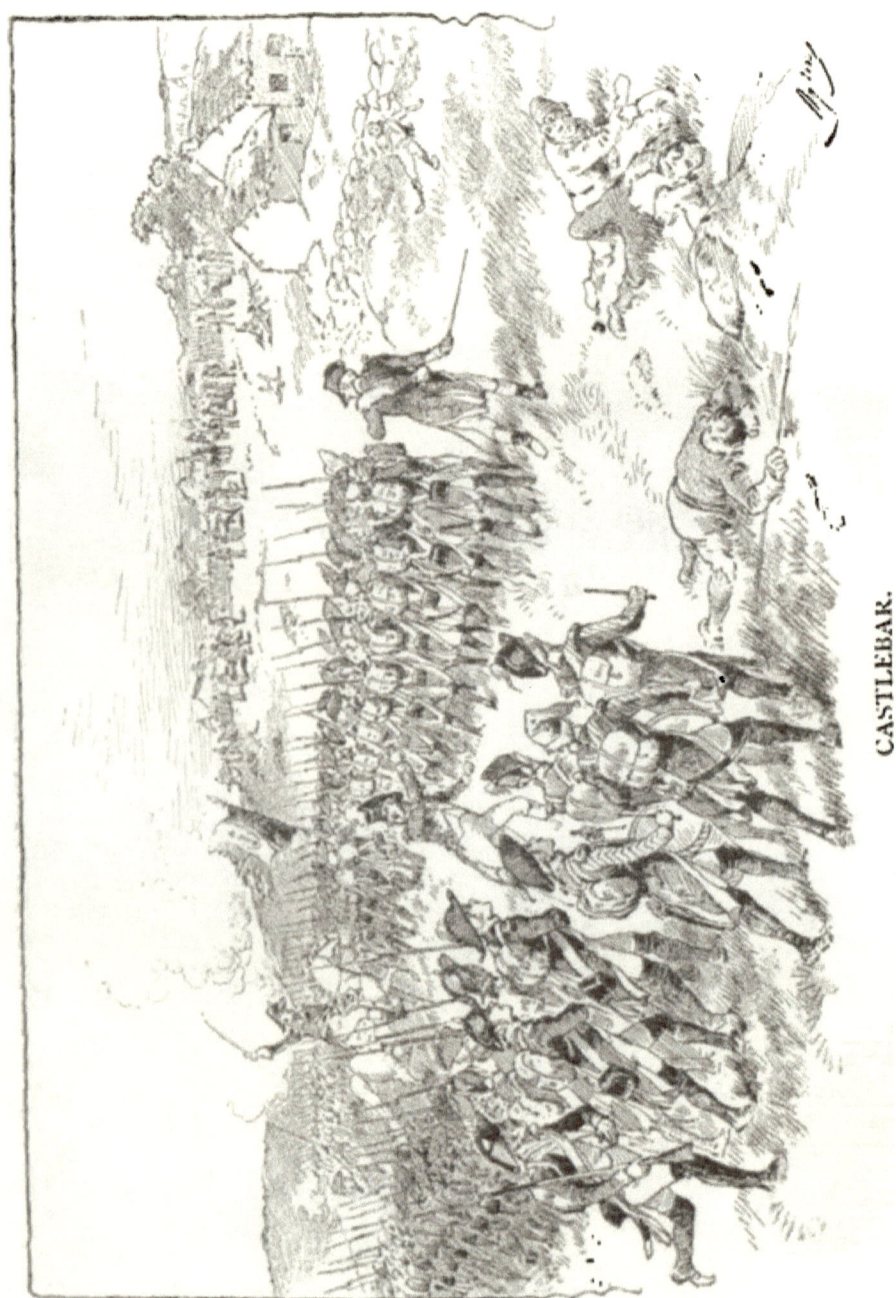

CASTLEBAR.

Valerian Gribayédoff

The French Invasion of Ireland in '98
Leaves of Unwritten History that Tell of an Heroic Endeavor and.....

ISBN/EAN: 9783337206208

Printed in Europe, USA, Canada, Australia, Japan

Cover: Foto ©ninafisch / pixelio.de

More available books at **www.hansebooks.com**

CONTENTS.

CHAPTER I.

CHAPTER II.

CHAPTER III.

CHAPTER IV.

CHAPTER V.

CHAPTER VI.

CHAPTER VII.

CHAPTER VIII.

CHAPTER IX.

LIST OF ILLUSTRATIONS.

AUTHORITIES.

Dublin Penny Journal. Dublin, 1833-34.

History of the Rebellion in Ireland. Rev. J. GORDON. London, 1801.

Rise and Fall of the Irish Nation. Sir JONAH BARRINGTON, 1815.

Memoirs of the Rebellion in Ireland. Sir R. MUSGRAVE. Dublin, 1801.

An Historical Review of the State of Ireland. FRANCIS PLOWDEN. Dublin, 1805.

Jones' Narrative of the Insurrection in Connaught. Reprint. Carlisle, Pa., 1805.

General Humbert's Official Reports to the Directory and the Marine Minister, 1798. Archives de France.

Le Moniteur Général. An vi. and vii.

Reports and Letters of Generals Lake, Trench, and Hutchinson. 1798.

A Narrative of What Passed at Killala. By an Eye-witness. London, 1800.

Notice Historique de la Déscente des Français en Irlande. L. O. FONTAINE. Paris, 1801.

Personal Narrative of the Irish Rebellion. C. H. TEELING. Belfast, 1832.

Saunders' Newsletter and Daily Advertiser. Dublin, 1798.

Parochial Survey of Ireland. M. W. MONK. Dublin, 1814.

Topographical Dictr. of Ireland. S. LEWIS. London, 1837.

Pieces of Irish History. W. J. MCNEVIN. New York, 1807.

Dissertations on the History of Ireland. C. O'CONNOR. Dublin, 1812.

Nouvelle Biographie Universelle. DIDOT. Paris, 1852.

Biographie Universelle. MICHAUD. Paris, 1843.

A New Biographical Dictionary. H. J. ROSE. London, 1848.

Correspondence of the Marquis of Cornwallis. London, 1859.

Resumen Historico de la Insurreccion de Nueva Espagna, desde su origen hasta el desembarco del Senor E. X. de Mina. Mexico, 1821.

Annuaire Nécrologique. Mahul. Année, 1823.

Thiers' History of the First Consulate and Empire.

Views of South America and Mexico. New York, 1826.

PREFACE.

THE present volume is an effort to rescue from comparative oblivion one of the many extraordinary episodes of the great French revolutionary war. Cortez and Pizarro, and scores of minor conquerors —nay, even buccaneers like Morgan—have found their panegyrists, but on the subject of General Humbert's descent upon Ireland in 1798 history is almost silent. Scarcely more than two years ago an English general—if I mistake not, Lord Wolseley— in a public speech referred to the " glorious fact that the United Kingdom had not been insulted by the presence of an armed invader since the days of William the Conqueror." The speaker's ignorance was excusable, seeing that the majority of English histories barely mention Humbert's name. None of them do justice to the magnitude of his achievements, or recount, in a manner worthy of the subject, the exploits which carried his small army to the very heart of Ireland.

Maxwell, in his *History of the Irish Rebellion*, rendered famous by a set of Cruikshank's illustrations, devotes one and a half chapters to the story of the expedition; but his narrative, being exclusively based on the official reports and the extremely partial account of the Tory writer, Sir Richard Musgrave (Dublin, 1801), the result is anything but satisfactory from a strictly historical point of view. For a similar reason does Mr. Froude's version of Humbert's descent, as contained in his recently published *History of Ireland*, prove superficial and inaccurate. Nor has the hardy Frenchman received better treatment from his own countrymen. Thiers dismisses him with six lines, and Guizot with the words: "A French invasion under command of General Humbert for a time gained some successes, owing to the incapacity or connivance of the Irish militia, but it was soon repulsed."

Two years of research, involving an examination of musty records and archives that have lain untouched in the British Museum and the Bibliothèque de France for almost a century, have convinced me that I am dealing with a case of historical oversight. Had Humbert's expedition not taken place at a period when the attention of Europe was riveted by Bonaparte and his schemes of Oriental conquest, the episode would doubtless have figured in history side by side with the "Bridge of Arcola," the passage of the St. Bernhard, the "Charge of the Light Brigade," and other popular traditions.

For what, in brief, were the circumstances under which the French landed in Ireland? Their entire strength fell short of 1,100 men of all arms, and on the day of their arrival at Killala the country was occupied by 150,000 English troops, thoroughly prepared for every emergency. For three weeks the invader held his own in the face of every difficulty, defeated several forces in the field—one, at the lowest computation, being *seven or eight times his superior in size*—conquered an entire province, and only surrendered to overwhelming odds after out-manœuvring the British commanders during an unremitting march of a week's duration. The French by that time had penetrated 150 miles into the interior of the country. As will be fully shown, Humbert's action was less quixotic than appears at first sight. An unfortunate delay of a few hours prevented his junction with a large body of Irish insurgents. Had he accomplished his purpose the road to Dublin would have been thrown open to him, and the history of Ireland might have been changed.

A word is perhaps apposite regarding several of the authorities I have consulted, a list of which will be found on pages 7 and 8. It is a habit of all chroniclers of the events of '98 who take the anti-English view to treat Sir Richard Musgrave's *Memoirs* as utterly unreliable. Musgrave, as a Tory

member of the Irish Parliament and an opponent
of Catholic emancipation, naturally allowed his partisan prejudices and religious convictions to color
his writings.   These teem with invective and denunciation against the rebels and the Catholic
clergy.   Nevertheless, a comparison of the *Me-*
moirs with other contemporaneous works on the
rebellion—even those of pro-Irish writers—fails, in
my opinion, to reveal any deliberate instance of
mendacity or fabrication on his part.   By reason
of his connection with the government he had
access to many channels of information closed to
the ordinary citizen, and in his copious appendix
will be found copies of the numerous sworn depo-
sitions upon which his charges against the rebels
are based.   Musgrave's principal sin is one of omis-
sion rather than commission, for he is ever careful
to pass over in silence the cruelties committed in
the name of the king and the constitution.   All
of which being the case, it is fair to assume that
his narrative, shorn of its animadversions, deserves
some consideration as an historical record.   With
all its faults, it helps to throw much light on the
events of the day, and I have not hesitated to refer
to it very frequently.

My most valuable authorities are a small work
entitled, *Jones' Narrative of the Insurrection in*
Connaught, of which a reprint was published in

Carlisle, Pa., in 1805,[1] and Louis Octave Fontaine's *Notice Historique de la Déscente des Français en Irlande* (Paris, 1801). The first-named book contains the narrations of several participants—active and passive—in those stormy events. Their style is simple but eloquent, and often dramatically descriptive. The absence of all striving for effect and partisan motive seems to stamp them with the seal of truth. On the merits of Fontaine's account I will not dwell at this stage, as a reference to the author is introduced into the story. As far as my personal investigations go, neither of these works has been previously consulted by any writer on the rebellion, and, in fact, it is a question whether more than one or two copies of them are now in existence.

For picturesque quality the French invasion of Ireland will stand comparison with the conquest of Mexico by Cortez. To Americans, in particular, the interest in the event will be enhanced by the fact that the hero died an American citizen on American soil, after gallantly serving his adopted country during the war of 1812. But apart from these considerations the story of Humbert's adventure points a moral that, amidst republican institutions like ours, will not fail to receive appreciation. It shows, on the one hand, the elevating influence

[1] A copy of this very rare work is in the author's possession.

of newly acquired liberties on a race ground down by centuries of feudalism and monarchical oppression, and, on the other, the debasing effects of religious and political intolerance both on the tyrant and his victim. For this reason mainly have I ventured on a domain that properly belongs to the military writer.

THE AUTHOR.

NEW YORK, *April 15, 1890.*

THE FRENCH INVASION OF IRELAND IN '98.

CHAPTER I.

The Events leading up to a French Invasion of Ireland—Several
Preliminary Attempts at an Invasion—Intrigues of the League
of United Irishmen—Outbreak of the Insurrection.

HE echoes of America's glorious revolution shook the old monarchies of Europe almost to their foundations. That of France soon succumbed to its effects. The year 1789 saw the abolition of the ancient *régime*, with its manifold abuses, and the dawn of a new independence that promised great things for the Old World. To what extent these prospects were marred by the excesses of demagogues and the mad infatuation of the multitude, history has sufficiently informed us; but there is no exaggeration in saying that with all the follies and crimes that marked its progress, that was the grandest epoch in France's history as a nation when five hundred thousand of her sons, ill-clad, half-starved and poorly drilled, faced the coalition of monarchical Europe in defence of their mother country and the republican idea. The watchword, " *la patrie en danger*," and the strains of Rouget de Lisle's inspiring battle hymn, made heroes out of the commonest clay. Men who had never smelled powder in their lives marched with light heart and steady tread against the well-disciplined foe. On the northern frontier it was the English and Austrians, on the western the Prussians, on the southern the Spaniards, who heard their ringing battle-cry and felt the prick of their cold steel. These ragged, unkempt *Sans-culottes*, not satisfied with hurling the enemy back over the frontiers, followed him into his own country. They overran the Rhine province and Belgium, and in the depth of winter crossed the frozen Dutch canals, driving the British before them like chaff; and, for the first time in the history of the world, a troop of cavalry captured a large fleet of powerful men-of-war, caught fast in the ice.

But notwithstanding her numerous successes on the field of battle, the odds continued to be enormously against the young republic. England's maritime power was making itself felt in an alarming degree. A cordon of British men-of-war, extending from Dunkirk to La Rochelle, and also the entire length of the Mediterranean seaboard, kept up an effectual blockade of every large port and deprived the French of their only means of replenishing a well-nigh exhausted exchequer. Every attempt to break the cordon, or even run the blockade, met with disaster, for, with all their bravery and devotion, the sailors of the republic were no match for the " tars of Old England." Inferior seamanship and lack of discipline, in fact, had resulted in an almost complete annihilation of the French navy.

In this dilemma the attention of the French Directory was turned toward Ireland as a potential ally. The story of Ireland's wrongs is a hackneyed theme nowadays, especially in America, and for that reason it has ceased to interest the majority of people. The writer must therefore be pardoned for indulging in a little sentiment anent the condition of that unhappy island, a prey alike to the exactions of the oppressor and the conflicting passions of the oppressed. Whatever may be said in extenuation of British methods in Ireland at the present time, testimony is not lacking to show that at the conclusion of the last century her grievances were numerous enough to justify the spirit of discontent which France found it to her interest to foster. The elective franchise was denied to all Catholics, and in consequence the major portion of the population were rendered indifferent to supporting laws in whose making they had no partici-

2

pation, and which neither benefited nor protected them. Protestations on the part of the disfranchised, accompanied too often by acts of lawlessness, only elicited the most stringent coercive measures; and at last there reigned a period of terror throughout the country which almost recalled the martyrdom of the Spanish Netherlands under Alva's bloody *régime*. The people in whole districts were required to remain within their houses from sunset to sunrise, and, to insure their doing so, visits were paid them during the hours of darkness. Woe betide the unfortunate man who had absented himself. He often returned to find his home in ashes. Nay, more—cases are known of persons merely suspected of treasonable offences being dragged from their beds, and, without the formalities of a trial or an effort to secure proof, being shot in cold blood or doomed to a lingering death amid the pestilential horrors of the prison ships. The infamous Insurrection Act provided the death penalty for all who even affiliated with secret societies; but, far from crushing the spirit of the patriots, who had organized themselves into the formidable "Order of United Irishmen," it served to bring them to a full realization of their desperate straits, and to brace their nerves for a final effort to throw off the galling yoke.[1]

[1] That the above statements are wholly unexaggerated may be gathered from the debates in the British House of Lords, November 22, 1797, on a motion by Lord Moira to petition his Majesty for the

As a natural result, the overtures of the French Directory for an alliance were eagerly accepted by the Executive Council of the Order, but with the express stipulation that no French invading army should exceed ten thousand men, and that Ireland, after her liberation, should be left free to enact her own laws and adopt her own form of government without foreign interference. The Directory having pledged its faith to these conditions, an armament was soon after equipped from the port of Brest under the command of General Lazare

intervention of the Crown in the affairs of Ireland. " My Lords," declared the speaker, " I have seen in Ireland the most absurd as well as the most disgusting tyranny that any nation ever groaned under. There is not one man, my Lords, in Ireland, who is not liable to be taken out of his house at any hour, either of the day or night, to be kept in rigorous confinement, restricted from all correspondence with the persons who have the management of his affairs, be treated with mixed severity and insult, and yet never know the crime with which he is charged, nor the source from whence the information against him proceeded. Your Lordships have, hitherto, detested the Inquisition. In what did that horrible institution differ from the system pursued in Ireland ? Men, indeed, have not been put to the rack in Ireland, because that horrible engine was not at hand. But I do know instances of men being picketed in Ireland till they fainted ; when they recovered, picketed again till they fainted ; recovered again, and again picketed till they fainted a third time ; and this in order to extort from the tortured sufferers a confession, either of their own guilt, or of the guilt of their neighbors. But I can even go farther : men have been half hanged and then brought to life, in order, by fear of having that punishment repeated, to induce them to confess the crimes with which they have been charged. . . . He who states these things should be prepared with proofs. I am prepared with them." . . .

Hoche, the hero of Weissenberg and Quiberon, and without contradiction one of the most promising leaders of the republican armies. Not yet thirty years of age, a man of keen insight, cool deliberation and iron will, ardently attached to democratic institutions, but withal averse to the acts of savagery that had attended their introduction into his own country, he seemed moulded by destiny for a great and glorious career. The liberation of Ireland, it should be added, had been his dream; he had urged it on the members of the Directory; he had dilated on it to his companions-in-arms. He based his argument on sentimental as well as political grounds. Ireland, he averred, that had supplied so many brave regiments to the armies of France, should be allowed to reap the benefits of the new republican era. The French armament, consisting of a fleet of 43 sail, carrying an army of 15,000 men and 40,000 stands of arms, also a formidable train of field artillery and heavy cannon, started from Brest in the month of December, 1796, and made for Bantry Bay, in the south of Ireland. Had this imposing force effected a landing, the result may be easily conjectured. How inadequate were England's preparations for her defence is evident from what occurred when the French did land eighteen months later. Suffice it to say that the special providence which, for good or for evil, has guarded England's shores since the day that the Spanish Armada went to pieces amid the waves of the English Channel, once more interposed, and after encountering one storm after the other, and failing entirely in the attempt to approach the Irish shore, the French fleet, somewhat battered, but without any material loss, returned to its moorings in the harbor of Brest.

The failure of the Bantry Bay expedition, while it proved a damper on the immediate hopes of the United Irishmen, in no manner discouraged them. Their emissaries in France continued to urge a renewal of the attempt, and pointed out the growing strength and cohesion of the brotherhood, with its ramifications extending to the remotest village in the land. Their efforts were partially successful, for in the following June the Batavian Republic, at the instance of the French Government, undertook to equip an armament for the purpose of carrying out General Hoche's project. Despite the reduced condition of her exchequer and the disorder in her military and naval departments, Holland was soon able to collect at the Texel sixteen sail of the line and a number of frigates, under the command of Admiral De Winter, with a landing force of thirteen thousand men, led by the intrepid Daendels, Commander-in-chief of the Batavian Army. This force practically constituted the entire disposable strength of the nation, and the willingness of the latter to devote it to the liberation of a suffering sister has been cited by enthusiasts as a case of national self-sacrifice, unprecedented in modern his-

tory.   Expectations in Ireland ran high, and many
longing eyes were directed toward the coast.   But
the patriots were doomed to fresh disappointment.
Weeks and months passed and the sail of the
deliverer appeared not.   Again had the elements
interposed themselves in England's favor.   All attempts to leave the Texel had been frustrated by
contrary winds, and after lying inactive for two
months the troops were disembarked, owing to a
scarcity of provisions, and the entire project was
abandoned.[1]

Almost simultaneously with the failure of the
Batavian expedition came the news to the Irish
Union of the death of General Hoche, their staunch
friend, and the expulsion of Carnot, the able or-
ganizer of the Bantry Bay expedition, from the
French Directory—and the realization of the United
Irishmen's dream seemed further off than ever!
At this juncture, however, their hopes were again
revived by the sudden conclusion of peace between
France and Austria, and the private assurance of
the Directory to the Union's emissaries that a fresh
effort in the direction of securing Ireland's independence would shortly be made.   This information, while giving confidence to the mass of the
brotherhood, was also the means of restraining their
impetuosity, which, had it taken the form of a pre-

[1] This Dutch fleet fell a prey to Lord Duncan and his heavy
" seventy-fours," in the memorable action off Camperdown, October
11, 1797.

mature outbreak, would have worked lasting injury to the cause. The spring of 1798 was the time set for the fulfilment of the Directory's promise, and to Bonaparte, the savior of Toulon and conqueror of Italy, was to be given the command of the new expeditionary army.

For the third time the British Government was filled with alarm, and the United Irishmen rejoiced. Every Briton capable of bearing arms was called upon by his sovereign to aid in the country's defence. The arsenals and ship-yards bustled with a feverish activity, and the well-fed shopkeepers and landed proprietors trembled for their homes and money-bags. But for a third time Fate was kind to Great Britain. Bonaparte was thinking of nothing so prosaic as a campaign amidst Irish bogs. His vivid Latin imagination had conjured up dreams of Oriental splendor. The entire East with its fascinating associations—in the foreground Egypt with her pyramids and sphinxes, then Palestine and Syria with their ancient ruins, and beyond that Hindustan with her untold wealth—these were the realms that seduced his fancy, and thither he sailed with the finest armament France had equipped in many a year!

The wail of disappointment and desperation that went up from Irish throats as the French fleet started for Egypt could scarcely fail to impress the British rulers, and to prepare them for coming events. Another circumstance tended to still fur-

ther open their eyes. Through the medium of its
spies the British Government discovered that emissaries of the Irish Union had deliberately thwarted
the negotiations for peace opened at Lille by Lord
Malmesbury, the English ambassador. These men
were found to be in intimate association with the
chiefs of the French Army, including Bernadotte,
Dessaix and Kilmaine, whose influence they used
to effect the rejection of all British overtures. The
presentation of the above facts in the Irish House
of Peers by the Lord Chancellor himself only
tended to accentuate the crisis. The policy of co-
ercion was followed up with redoubled vigor, the
object of the ministry—as has been charged—being
to drive the nation into armed rebellion, which
would serve as a pretext for depriving it of its last
vestige of independence. The plan, if such an one
was intended, succeeded only too well. Goaded on
by the arbitrary acts of the military leaders, who,
without the slightest authority of law, took it upon
themselves to supersede the ordinary tribunals of
justice and to try by court-martial citizens accused
of mere civil offences, the members of the League
at last threw off all restraint, and in the month of
May, 1798, broke out in open rebellion, first in the
neighborhood of Dublin, then in Kildare, Wexford
and Wicklow, and finally in Ulster.

It is not my purpose to dilate on the horrors that
followed. Each side vied with the other in barbarity and disregard of all human rights. But com-

mon justice requires that this distinction be made: whereas the rebels were, for the greater part, ignorant and fanatic peasants, conscious only of the grievous wrongs they had suffered, and therefore in a certain degree excusable for their acts, no such excuse can be offered for the disciplined troops of his Majesty, and, above all, for the Protestant Anglo-Irish militia, who richly deserve the reprobation of all ages for a degree of bloodthirstiness unparalleled in the history of modern warfare. For months the revolted provinces remained a prey to the conqueror, and scenes of devastation and rapine were of daily occurrence. The League of United Irishmen was practically a thing of the past, and the iron hand of the despot seemed to hold the stricken land tighter than ever in its deadly grasp. It was at this supreme hour of misery that the electrifying news sped through hill and dale, through town and hamlet, that a French army had landed at Killala, in the province of Connaught, and was on the march to deliver Ireland from the oppressor!

CHAPTER II.

HE town of Killala is situated on the bay of the same name, on the coast of County Mayo. It is an ancient bishop's see, and was founded in almost prehistoric times by Amhley, a prince of the district, who, according to tradition, was converted by St. Patrick, together with seven hundred of his subjects, in a single day. In 1798 there still remained some relics of a bygone age. Among them were the ruins of a "round tower," erected in the sixth century by the eminent Irish architect and divine, Gobhan, on a knoll in the centre of the town. From the base of this elevation three roads diverged—the main street taking an easterly direction, winding by the church-yard wall, down a steep hill to the bishop's castle, another aged structure dating back many centuries, that but for constant repair would long since have crumbled into decay; a second road running south to the "Acres," a distant height on the border of the town; and a third pursuing a westerly course to the banks of the Owenmore, two miles away. This river is crossed by a majestic stone bridge of eleven arches at the village of Parsontown, from which point the road branches east, following the windings of the stream for nearly a mile; then bending north-west parallel to the Bay of Rathfran—an inlet of the Bay of Killala—it merges into the highway of Foghill. On the banks of a creek at the western extremity of the Bay of Rathfran stand the moss-grown ruins of Kilcummin, a cell built by Cumin in the seventh century.

It was within sight of this romantic spot that, early in the afternoon of the 22d of August, 1798, several fishermen, while busy repairing their nets, were surprised by the appearance of three large war-ships suddenly rounding a neighboring promontory and casting anchor two hundred feet from the shore. For some days past vague rumors had floated through the air that a French fleet had left La Rochelle and was on its way to the Irish coast. At first sight, therefore, the men decided that this must be the enemy. But a second glance revealed the British colors flying at the vessels' bows, and, eager to earn a few pennies, they left their work and at a brisk gait crossed the high ground that hid

the bay from the town of Killala. Reaching this
place they made a straight line for the dwelling of
the Rev. Dr. Joseph Stock, Protestant bishop of
Killala, and in all respects the leading inhabitant
of that section of the country. This excellent man,
in spite of his intense Protestantism and fealty
to the government, harbored a deep resentment
toward the ultra-loyalists, whose machinations were
furnishing a plausible pretext to the Romanists
for distrust and hostility toward their Protestant
brethren in general. Orange lodges for the avowed
purpose of stirring up strife were being started in
Connaught, and the bishop was opposing them
with might and main. On this very day he was
busied in entering a protest, in his "primary visita-
tion" charge, against the first sentence of the oath
by which Orangemen are banded together, *viz.*: " I
am not a Roman Catholic." To his broad and liberal mind such a sentiment had too pharisaical a
ring. It sounded too much like: "Stand off, I am
holier than thou ! "[1]

Greatly pleased were the reverend gentleman
and his guests—clergymen from the vicinity—at
the news brought by the fishermen. A British
fleet in the bay meant an end to all danger from
the French. It meant an end to the condition of
suspense into which the Protestant population had
been thrown by the persistent rumors from all
sides. Even among the servants in the bishop's

[1] *Narrative of What Passed at Killala.*

"The three stately ships in the foreground, and the verdant, undulating hillocks bordering the shore beyond, formed a charming picture."

—Page 29

household the belief had been firm that something unusual was impending. A Protestant servant-maid, married to a Catholic, suspected of affiliation with the rebels, had circulated the report, and Mr. William Kirkwood, the local magistrate, had in so far credited it as to keep under arms, as a precautionary measure, the entire body of yeomanry under his command, together with the Prince of Wales' Fencibles under Lieutenant Sills—numbering about fifty men, say the loyalist writers, but numbering many more, say other authorities.[1]

Impelled by a desire to pay their respects to the officers of the squadron—possibly also to extend the hospitalities of the castle—the bishop's two sons, Edwin and Arthur Stock, ran down to the wharf and jumped into a fishing boat. Here they were joined by the port surveyor, Mr. James Rutledge, and a few minutes later the three were skimming over the placid surface of the bay on their way to the men-of-war. It was nearly three o'clock, and the sun beat on the water with a fierce, white glare. The three stately ships in the foreground, and the verdant, undulating hillocks bordering the shore beyond, formed a charming picture. As the small boat came within hailing distance Rutledge commented on the peculiar construction of the vessels, all three apparently frigates. His surprise was increased at the sight

[1] Adjutant-General Louis Octave Fontaine, for instance, estimates the British force at two hundred men.—*Notice Historique*, p. 7.

of a number of minor craft plying to and from the shore, laden with blue-coated soldiers, who formed in line at a short distance from the water's edge. Still suspecting nothing, the three approached the nearest war ship, from the bows of which numerous shaggy heads stared expectantly.

"Nice-looking fellows for. British man-of-war's men!" remarked Rutledge, derisively.

His hailing cry was answered in a deep bass voice, with an unmistakable Irish brogue. A rope ladder was lowered, and the three men were hoisted on deck. But what was their astonishment to find, in lieu of a natty British captain and crew, a row of gaunt and sallow men in the uniform of the French army, one of whom stepped forward and informed them, in good Dublin English, and in the name of his superior, General Jean-Joseph Humbert, there present, that they were on board the French frigate *Concorde*, prisoners of war in the hands of France.

The prolonged absence of the bishop's sons and the surveyor soon awoke suspicions in the minds of the loyalists of Killala. By four o'clock the excitement was at fever heat. The inhabitants had gathered on Steeple Hill, where Captain Kirkwood with his corps, in full uniform, were awaiting the issue of events. Two officers from the garrison of Ballina, eight miles away, who had seen service at the Cape of Good Hope and were judges on matters naval and military, were eagerly interrogated by the spectators, but they could form no authoritative opinion as to the nature of the vessels. " Here," said Captain Kirkwood, handing his telescope to an old denizen of the town who had fought under Howe and Rodney, " here, tell me what these vessels are." " They are French, sir," returned the sea-dog. " I know them by the cut and color of their sails." Turning to leave the crowd, Captain Kirkwood was questioned by Neal Kerugan (a noisy malcontent, and afterward a leader of the insurgents) as to the nationality of the frigates. " Ah, Neal," replied the captain, significantly, " you know as well as I do."

Just about this time a peasant covered with dust and sweat rode furiously into Parsontown with the startling information that troops in blue uniforms were landing from the ships, and were distributing arms to many of the inhabitants who had joined them. Presently this fact was confirmed when a solid body of men were descried moving along the road leading to Killala. Now hidden in the hollows, now sharply outlined against the sky, their arms flashing in the rays of the setting sun, they marched slowly but steadily onward, preceded by a single horseman—a large, robust-looking man, dressed in a long green hunting frock and a huge conical fur cap. On meeting parties of the townsfolk he stopped and saluted them in the Leinster patois: " *Go de mu ha tu* " (How do you do). Close upon his heels rode a French general—Sarrazin—and his aide-de-camp, one Matthew Tone, both seemingly much amused at the other's successful handling of the Irish tongue. When they had crossed the Parsontown bridge General Humbert drove up in a gig and ordered three hundred of his men to bivouac on the green esplanade in front of the village, while the remainder were sent on to Killala.

Twilight was falling on the world, and the gentle voices of the evening insects were singing a lullaby to the drowsy earth when Sarrazin's stalwart grenadiers and infantry marched down the hill of Mullaghern and advanced upon the little town. Captain Kirkwood, informed of the true state of affairs, hastily gathered together his yeomanry and the Fencibles, and ordered them to a commanding ridge on the outskirts; but soon deciding this position to be less advantageous than one within the town itself, he fell back and took a stand at the top of the decline leading to the castle. He showed his wisdom, for no better situation could have been selected for a retreat. Sarrazin, on arriving within gunshot of the enemy, made his dispositions. He sent a detachment under Neal Kerugan—now a full-fledged rebel —to occupy the "Acres" road, to turn the British, if in position, or cut them off in the event of their retreating. He stationed a handful of sharpshooters on the deserted ridge, and sent the green-coated horseman referred to before forward to reconnoitre. Through the winding streets the chasseur dashed. The target of many a bullet, he reached the market-place unharmed. Here he was challenged by a young gentleman of the place in yeoman's uniform with: "What do you want, you spy?" The voice of war is the scream of the bullet, and the answer, conveyed through the medium of a pistol, was both convincing and silencing. One more dash in the face of death to inspect the enemy's position, and this modern Achilles, with *his* heel well booted, was back among his companions, where he related with much unction that "though he had been in twenty battles, he had never before had the honor to receive the entire fire of the enemy's lines."[1]

By this time the action had begun. The sharp-shooters were showing their mettle, and the grenadiers, who had headed the attacking column, deployed on the main street, in the centre of the town. There they were opposed by the English with a faint-hearted fire. Captain Kirkwood, alarmed at the indecision of his men, ordered them in excited tones to charge. The command found no response. The line hesitated, wavered, broke— and in a moment the whole force were skurrying toward the castle gates. In the scramble the town's apothecary, a respectable citizen of the name of Smith, was laid low by a bullet from a French trooper, and the Rev. Dr. Ellison, of Castlebar, an

---

[1] This interesting episode is gleaned from the account of an eye-witness published in the *Dublin Penny Journal* of 1833. The name of the hero is unfortunately not mentioned, but the man was probably Henry O'Keon, one of the prominent Irish members of the expedition.

Anglican clergyman and guest of the bishop, who
had bravely appeared in the ranks, musket in hand,
received a wound in the heel.   At the castle gates
the fight was resumed, this time with some spirit.
The defenders endeavored to barricade the entrance,
but notwithstanding the unquestionable bravery of
their commanders, one of whom, Lieutenant Sills,
wounded an officer of the attacking party, the gate
was forced open and what remained of the British
laid down their arms.   These were nineteen in
number.   The rest had been killed or wounded, or
had fled.   Among the latter were the two officers
from Ballina, who carried the news to their commander.

An interesting scene occurred when the smoke
in the court-yard had cleared away.   A tall man of
resolute mien, wearing a general's epaulettes, who
arrived at the conclusion of the fight, accompanied
by a numerous staff, and who proved to be Humbert himself, suddenly ordered the troops in stento-
rian tones to ground arms.   Then turning to the
three prisoners, Mr. Rutledge and the Stock boys,
who had been brought with the column, he asked
through an interpreter where the bishop could be
found.   Naturally the badly frightened men were
unable to supply the information; but the suspense
was of short duration, for presently the worthy prelate emerged from the bushes of his garden near
by.   He was at once assured by the same interpreter, one Bartholomew Teeling—of whom there

will be occasion to speak further on—that no harm was intended ; and as he stepped forward Humbert extended his hand. What improved matters was the bishop's knowledge of French, an advantage which, combined with his honest exterior, impressed the general favorably. At all events the latter's first words breathed kindness and good will.

" Take my word for it," was his assurance, " that neither your people' nor yourself shall have cause to feel any apprehension. We have come to your country not as conquerors, but as deliverers, and shall take only from you absolutely what is necessary for our support. You are as safe under our protection as you were under that of his Majesty, the King of England."

All contemporaneous authorities, be they English or Irish, loyalist or revolutionist, agree that, to the honor of the French name, this promise was religiously kept. History furnishes few examples of so scrupulous an observance of the rules of civilized warfare, so thorough a respect for the rights of the conquered, as distinguished the operations of General Humbert and his little army.

And now a few words regarding the origin and organization of this expedition, which for a short period threatened to crush out England's supremacy in the Emerald Isle. In the preceding chapter reference was made to the several isolated attempts on the part of the French Directory to

land an invading army on the Irish coast. The last
one had been balked by Bonaparte's designs on
Egypt. Thereafter the demands for aid of the
Irish emissaries in Paris only became more urgent
and incessant. Owing to the Egyptian expedition
having well nigh drained the republic of money,
ships and stores, several months elapsed before a
fresh armament could be equipped. This time it
was decided to send out two small advance forces,
and to follow them up later with a main body. For
that end General Humbert was stationed at La
Rochelle with about 1,000 veterans, while General
Hardy took up quarters at Brest with 3,000 soldiers,
mainly ex-convicts. The *gros* of the expeditionary
force, numbering 10,000 men, was placed under the
orders of "*Kilmaine le brave*," as his companions-in-
arms delighted to call him. This distinguished
officer was an Irishman by birth, named Jennings,
who assumed the "*nom de guerre*" of Kilmaine
upon entering the French military service, where
his splendid achievements on the frontier of the
Austrian Netherlands elevated him to the rank of
lieutenant-general.

Of these three separate forces only the smallest,
under the orders of Humbert, was destined to reach
its goal. Humbert himself, if some of his biog-
raphers are to be believed, was far from being the
ideal hero of a romance of war. To his many brilliant parts were allied vices that in any but a dis-
organized state of society must have disqualified

him for every position of honor. Beset as she was
at that epoch with enemies on all her borders,
France had need for every citizen who could con-
tribute to the salvation of the fatherland. Purity
of character was little in demand, and the man of
ability, however unscrupulous, possessed better
chances of advancement than his honest but mediocre neighbor. The authorities are divided both
as to Humbert's birth-place and the date of his
birth.[1] From one source we learn that he was born
at Rouveroye, November 25, 1755; from another
that he first saw the light of day in 1767 at Bouvron
(Meurthe). But this is a small matter. It appears
to be beyond dispute that young Jean-Joseph
Amable Humbert was a " hard character " from the
very start, and that he brought much sorrow on his
grandmother, on whom the care of the youth devolved after the early death of both his parents.
After leading her a life of misery, he left her roof at
the age of seventeen to enter the service of a cloth
merchant in a neighboring town. He had shown
an early disposition to pay undue attentions to the
fair sex, and his handsome face and lithesome figure
had stood him in good stead in these matters.
Away from home the temptation grew stronger,
and we soon find him dismissed from his employ
for acts of gross immorality. The youth returned

[1] See Didot's *Biographie Universelle*, Paris, 1852 ; Michaud's
Biographie Universelle, Paris. 1848; Le Bas' *Encyclopædie Bio-
graphique*, Paris, 1853.

to Rouveroye,[1] but his reputation had preceded
him, and he saw every door closed at his coming.

For the second time he left home to seek his for-
tunes elsewhere, and again, as before, his ill-conduct
brought with it a summary dismissal from a steady
situation in a hat factory in Lyons. The young
man now became a social pariah. These were still
ante-revolutionary times, and a disgraced *employé*
found it difficult to secure recognition anywhere.
Starvation stared our hero in the face. In this
dilemma a happy thought struck him. He had cas-
ually discovered that skins of certain animals, such
as rabbits, young goats, etc., were in great demand
in the glove and leggings factories of Lyons and
Grenoble. He therefore started out with a few
francs in his pockets, and wandering among the
remote villages of the Vosges district, purchased at
low rates as much of this merchandise as his means
would allow. A handsome profit on the first batch
encouraged him to undertake a second and a third
tour, and after awhile his figure became familiar
throughout a large tract of the country.

At last there resounded the tocsin of the great
revolution. For once the heart of the wanderer
seems to have throbbed with a grand impulse. The
fires of ambition that had lain dormant in his breast
blazed forth in all their fury. Abandoning his now
prosperous pursuits, he threw himself into the great

---

[1] The weight of evidence is in favor of Rouveroye as the birth-
place of Humbert.

movement. Peasants who had bartered and bargained with him, maidens who had known him as a peripatetic swain, were electrified by the earnestness of his exhortations. He joined one of the first volunteer battalions organized among the Vosges, and by his active republicanism no less than by his military qualities, quickly rose to be its chief. With the rank of *Maréchal-de-camp*, he accompanied the army under Beurnonville which in 1793 burst into the territory of Trèves. It was here that another bad side to his character disclosed itself. On the field of battle brave to a fault, utterly regardless of his own person and ever ready to embark in the most perilous enterprise, in camp he proved himself an arch intriguer. Anxious to secure promotion, he secretly sought permission from the Directory to act as an informer on the movements of his comrades-in-arms, averring that many were guilty of lukewarmness in the cause of the republic. Beurnonville, however, got wind of his subordinate's schemes, and wrote a scathing letter of denunciation to the military authorities in Paris, characterizing the action as the height of baseness (*le comble de la scélératesse*) on Humbert's part, and demanding his immediate recall.

Concluding a *modus vivendi* between the two to be henceforth out of the question, the Directory reluctantly acceded to Beurnonville's request, and for some months Humbert prowled around Jacobin headquarters in Paris, awaiting fresh employment.

His persuasive eloquence and apparent earnestness as a promoter of republican doctrine made him a favorite there. In April, 1794, he was promoted general of brigade and given a command in the Army of the West. Of all the different forces sent out to combat the enemies of the republic, that which opposed the fierce *chouans* of La Vendée encountered the greatest dangers and obstacles. Victor Hugo, in his *Légende des Siècles*, has fittingly described the struggle as a combat "'twixt the soldiers of light and the heroes of darkness;" and in truth, were it not for the atrocities committed on both sides, this campaign might take its place among the most brilliant annals of ancient chivalry. Neither party asked nor expected quarter. It was a war to the knife, without truce, without respite. Humbert showed himself equal to every emergency. He hunted down the foe with unabating ardor, tracked him into his marshy lairs and forest fastnesses, and won the admiration of the entire army by his personal disregard of danger. After many months of hard fighting, the Convention decided to adopt a milder course toward the insurgents, and on March 7, 1795, a treaty was signed at Nantes by which, in return for certain privileges, the Vendeans agreed to acknowledge the republic. The pause in hostilities was unfortunately of short duration. Cormatin-Desoteux, the *chouan* leader, having repeatedly violated several provisions of the treaty, Humbert effected his arrest, and sent him in chains to Cherbourg.

This act, coupled with the discovery of a traitorous correspondence between the Vendean leaders and the English Government, fanned the smouldering embers of factional hatred, and by the beginning of summer the civil war was renewed with increased ferocity.

As second in command under General Hoche, Humbert took part in all the operations at Quiberon against the Anglo-Emigrant Army landed by a British fleet. He inflicted a crushing defeat on the invaders on July 16th, from behind his entrenchments at St. Barbe, and on the 20th stormed the fort of Penthièvre, thereby destroying or capturing the entire emigrant force. The subsequent massacre of prisoners, which will ever remain a blot on the escutcheon of the republic, is, however, not to be laid at his door. The horrible act was ordered by the two General Commissaries, Blad and Tallien, and was executed against the wishes both of Hoche and Humbert. The latter had not made himself popular among the Moderatists while in Paris, and the opportunity was seized upon by the newspapers of the Clichy party to hold him up to public contempt. His early vocation was thrown up against him, and the former "*marchand de peaux de lapin*" became the target of many a satire in prose and verse. All these assaults were fruitless, however. If anything, they tended to cement his influence with the Directory. In any case he was made a general of division, and selected, a

year after, to accompany Hoche in the expedition
to Ireland. Reference has already been made to
this event, and to the failure of the French to
effect a landing. One of their ships, the *Droits de
l'Homme*, a seventy-four, was intercepted on the
retreat by two English vessels, and between their
cross-fire and the raging of a terrific storm, she was
completely wrecked. Of the 1,800 men on board,
barely 400 escaped with their lives, and among
these was General Humbert.

Such was the career of the man upon whom now
devolved the task of bearding the British lion in his
den. To complete the picture one cannot do better than quote the following estimate of his character, contained in an anonymous pamphlet published in 1800, the authorship of which has been
brought home to Bishop Stock, of Killala:[1]

"Humbert, the leader of this singular body of
men," says the writer, "was himself as extraordinary a personage as any in his army. Of a good
height and shape, in the full vigor of life, prompt
to decide, quick in execution, apparently master of
his art, you could not refuse him the praise of a
good officer, while his physiognomy forbade you to
like him as a man. His eye, which was small and
sleepy (the effect, probably, of much watching),
cast a sidelong glance of insidiousness, and even of
cruelty : it was the eye of a cat preparing to spring
upon her prey. His education and manners were

[1] *A Narrative of What Passed at Killala.* By an Eye-witness.

indicative of a person sprung from the lower order of society, though he knew how (as most of his countrymen can do) to assume, where it was convenient, the deportment of a gentleman. For learning he had scarcely enough to enable him to write his name. His passions were furious, and all his behavior seemed marked with the characters of roughness and violence. A narrower observation of him, however, served to discover that much of this roughness was the result of art, being assumed with the view of extorting by terror a ready compliance with his commands."

Prior to his embarkation from La Rochelle Humbert had difficulties of no trifling nature to contend with. As stated, France's resources had been sorely taxed by the expedition to Egypt, and neither money nor even necessaries for the troops could be obtained from the Commissariat Department. Yet no obstacle could daunt the indomitable spirit of the soldier., Hoche was no more, but the same determination to strike a blow at England's vital point controlled the actions of his friend and successor. Impatient of delay, and refusing longer to await the coöperation of others, Humbert and his slender detachment put to sea on the morning of August 4th, at seven o'clock. The event occasioned much enthusiasm in La Rochelle, and the quays were thronged with citizens who shouted themselves hoarse in bidding god-speed to the " Army of Ireland." A powerful English fleet was cruising within a mile of the port, and it required great skill on the part of Division Commander Daniel Savary to escape a conflict. Only by plying vigorously to the windward did he succeed. It had been decided in advance that rather than accept battle against the tremendous odds the three vessels should be run aground on the Spanish coast.[1]

Humbert's armament consisted of three frigates: the *Concorde* and *Medée*, of 44 eighteen-pounders each, and the *Franchise*, of 38 twelve-pounders. His entire landing strength did not exceed 1,060 rank and file and 70 officers, with two pieces of field artillery, four-pounders. He also brought 5,500 stands of arms for the arming of the Irish peasantry.[2] His troops were composed in the main of infantry of the line, with two companies of grenadiers and a squadron of the Third Regiment of Chasseurs. All were veterans and had seen service under Jourdan and Moreau on the Rhine, or under Bonaparte in Italy.

The officers, some of whom bore on their persons the marks of many a bloody encounter, deserve a preliminary notice. There was Sarrazin, to

[1] Fontaine's *Notice Historique.*

[2] These figures are from Sir Richard Musgrave's *Memoirs* and other authentic sources. However, according to Fontaine, Humbert's adjutant-general, the total strength amounted to but 1,032 men, *viz.* : the second battalion of the 70th Half-Brigade, 45 *Chasseurs à Cheval* belonging to the Third Regiment, 42 coast-guard gunners, and 50 officers. See Fontaine's *Notice Historique*, page 2.

GENERAL SARRAZIN.

begin with, a remarkable figure in his way, whose career, like Humbert's, may be considered thoroughly illustrative of the peculiar conditions created in the military system of France by the change in her political life. Born in 1770, the third year of the revolution already saw him a captain of infantry. In 1794 he was transferred to the Engineers, but shortly after, in consequence of prowess in the field, received his commission as colonel of the Fourteenth Regiment of Dragoons. In 1796 he was already a general-adjutant, and, as will soon be shown, the " Irish Campaign " brought him further promotion. Sarrazin, in other words, was the true type of the French Republican soldier: a product of those troublesome and stormy times when success meant rapid rise to honors and distinctions, and failure—the gory embrace of the guillotine![1] Next in authority after Sarrazin came Adjutant-General Louis Octave Fontaine, to whose pen the author is indebted for a remarkable account of the expedition. His book, or pamphlet, was published in Paris two years after the event, and although it teems with errors, geographical, chronological and others, it is valuable as the only authentic French version in existence, outside of General Humbert's meagre reports to the Directory. The writer constantly refers to himself in the

[1] These particulars are from a periodical entitled *The Philosopher*, edited by Sarrazin himself while an exile in London some years later.

third person as "*le brave Général Fontaine*," and
would have us believe that the partial success of
the invasion was due to his own foresight and
energy.   With a *naïveté* refreshing for its very
frankness, he places himself in the light of a
Deus ex machina, ever turning up at the right moment to extricate his companions from dire dilemmas and show them the road to victory.   This
naïveté attains its pinnacle when, as if by an after-
thought, he explains at the conclusion of his work
that he has purposely omitted mentioning the
names of his companions-in-arms for fear of over-
looking any one of them and thus causing un-
merited pain.   The fatuous vanity of the writer,
and his unfortunate habit of treating Irish names
and places as unworthy of proper record, does not
prevent his furnishing many a missing link to
the chain of evidence touching this extraordinary
phase of modern history, and for so much, if for
no other reason, posterity must feel grateful to
him.

   Several Irishmen accompanied Humbert in various capacities.   Bartholomew Teeling, of Lisburn,
was one.   He was a young man who had left his
native country—a mere stripling—to join the
French Republican Army.   He had fought side by
side with rabid atheists and open enemies of the
Church, and yet through all these experiences his
faith in the religion of his forefathers had never
slackened.   A scholar, a patriot and an observer,

with an admixture of the enthusiast, he had not
allowed his political convictions to interfere with
his religious belief. His mildness of manner and
patrician bearing formed a pleasing contrast to the
rough, soldier-like deportment of Humbert, who
had selected him as his aide-de-camp. Humbert's
official interpreter was another Irishman, one Henry
O'Keon, the son of a cow-herd of Lord Tyrawley.
He was born in the neighborhood of Kilcummin,
the landing-place of the French near Killala—a circumstance which points its own conclusion and re-
futes the oft-repeated statement that that spot had
been selected by mere chance. Having learned a
little Latin at school, O'Keon repaired to Nantes,
Brittany, where he studied theology and received
holy orders. On the advent of the republic he
suddenly changed his convictions—if indeed he had
ever entertained any—enlisted in the army as a
private, and was gradually advanced to the rank of
major. He was physically well developed and
possessed the heavy, coarse features of the lower
type of the Celtic race. The merry twinkle of
his eyes and the joviality of his ruddy counte-
nance completely dispelled the repellent effect of a
pair of heavy, beetling eyebrows. He spoke Irish
and French fluently, and English indifferently.
His part in the campaign was a creditable one,
and would entitle him to an honorable place in
its history had he not marred it by an act of
dishonesty toward the Bishop of Killala, and a

breach of good morals, before his final departure for France.[1]

Two other Irishmen accompanied the expedition —Matthew Tone, already mentioned, brother of the celebrated Theobald Wolfe Tone, and one O'Sullivan, a native of South Ireland and one of the very few rebel leaders who were fortunate enough to escape the avenging hand of the British Government. Although captured by the loyalists, he was not recognized, and afterward made his way back to the continent.

[1] He swindled Bishop Stock out of twelve guineas and took away with him from Dublin another man's wife.—*Narrative of What Passed at Killala.*

CHAPTER III.

S the last rays of the setting sun illumined the town and bay of Killala on that memorable 22d of August, 1798, a French soldier climbed to the roof of the Episcopal palace and lowered the British colors that from time immemorial had floated there. The staff was not destined to remain long bare, for presently a green flag, with a harp embroidered in the centre, and bearing the motto, " *Erin go Bragh*," rose slowly from its base, greeted by a triple salvo and the cheers of a large concourse of people. The inhabitants of Killala had fully realized the significance of the situation, and the large majority being malcontents, the invading army had been surrounded by enthusiastic throngs, eager to offer help and coöperation.

4

To what extent the leaders of the insurgents
were prepared for Humbert's coming may be gathered from the somewhat colored statement of a
loyalist inhabitant, who declares that a number of
them appeared from the start in uniforms provided
by their " *new* friends." " Nothing," he continues,
"could exceed the consternation which prevailed
throughout the town—the loyalists every moment
expecting to be butchered in cold blood. Men,
women and children, drowned in tears, attempted
to escape, but in vain. Every avenue leading from
Killala was thronged by rebels making in to receive
the fraternal embrace, whose eyes indicated the
malignity of their hearts. No one was permitted
to depart but on business which concerned the invaders." [1]

Humbert was not dilatory in arranging for the
provisioning of his troops. His supplies had run
short, owing to the hurry of his departure from La
Rochelle, and he had no reason to expect any further help for the present from France.[2] So the
very evening of his arrival he ordered the prisoners
to be brought before him and questioned them
closely as to the resources of the district. He

[1] *Jones' Narrative* (Am. reprint), page 282.

[2] Here is Adjutant-General Fontaine's reflection on this subject
(See his *Notice Historique*, page 6): " Nous avions à bord des
provisions à bouche, c'est-à-dire, quelques sacs de biscuits, et une
pipe d'eau-de-vie. On jugera par ce détail exact que nous nous
étions plus occupés de la gloire que des moyens d'assurer notre
existence."

assured the bishop, however, that while the necessities of war would compel him to requisition a certain number of horses and cattle, he intended eventually to compensate the owners, who would in the meanwhile receive vouchers for all such property, payable on the Irish Directory, shortly to be established in Connaught. Magistrate Kirkwood's answers to the different interrogatories, as interpreted by Teeling, were apparently so frank and truthful that Humbert took a fancy to him, and, placing him on parole, assured him that he would be entirely unmolested and allowed to attend to his private affairs, provided he remained within the town's limits. Unhappily for the magistrate, his invalid wife had meanwhile fled to the neighboring mountains, and his anxiety for her welfare resulted in his starting out in search of her the very next day. Of course this action was regarded as a flagrant breach of parole, and in retaliation the French helped themselves freely to everything they could find in his house. They also permitted the Irish revolutionists to ransack it from top to bottom, so that Kirkwood subsequently returned to find his home a ruin.

But if one excepts a little sally of ill-humor on Humbert's part when he discovered, the day after the landing, that the bishop had failed to comply with the orders for furnishing horses and cattle, the treatment of Kirkwood was the only approach to severity that can be laid at the door of the

French during their entire stay in Ireland. If we are to believe the bishop himself—and he certainly could have no motive for exaggerating the virtues of the invaders of his country—the discipline maintained by Humbert's troops was excellent throughout. "With every temptation to plunder," he remarks, "which the time and the number of valuable articles within their reach presented to them in the bishop's palace, from a sideboard of plate and glasses, a hall filled with hats, whips, and great-coats, as well of the guests as of the family, not a single particular of private property was found to have been carried away when the owners, after the first fright was over, came to look for their effects, which was not for a day or two after the landing. Immediately upon entering the dining-room a French officer had called for the bishop's butler, and gathering up the spoons and glasses had desired him to take them to his pantry. Beside the entire use of other apartments during the stay of the French in Killala, the attic story, containing a library and three bed-chambers, continued sacred to the bishop and his family. And so scrupulous was the delicacy of the French not to disturb the female part of the house, that not one of them was ever seen to go higher than the middle floor, except on the evening of their success at Castlebar, when two officers begged leave to carry to the family the news of the battle, and seemed a little mortified that the intelligence was received with an air of dissatisfaction."

On the morning of the 23d the French commander issued a proclamation that had been carefully prepared by himself and the Irish officers accompanying the expedition. It was couched in the florid language of the day, and, translated into the Irish tongue, was well calculated to stir the fervid Celtic nature to action. It read as follows:

LIBERTY, EQUALITY, FRATERNITY, UNION !

IRISHMEN :

You have not forgotten Bantry Bay—you know what efforts France has made to assist you. Her affections for you, her desire for avenging your wrongs and insuring your independence, can never be impaired.

After several unsuccessful attempts, behold Frenchmen arrived amongst you.

They come to support your courage, to share your dangers, to join their arms and to mix their blood with yours in the sacred cause of liberty! They are the forerunners of other Frenchmen, whom you shall soon enfold in your arms.

Brave Irishmen, our cause is common; like you, we abhor the avaricious and bloodthirsty policy of an oppressive government; like you, we hold as indefensible the right of all nations to liberty; like you, we are persuaded that the peace of the world shall ever be troubled as long as the British Ministry is suffered to make with impunity a traffic of the industry, labor and blood of the people.

But exclusive of the same interests which unite us, we have powerful motives to love and defend you.

Have we not been the pretext of the cruelty exercised against you by the Cabinet of St. James? The heartfelt interest you have shown in the grand events of our revolution—has it not been imputed to you as a crime? Are not tortures

and death continually hanging over such of you as are barely
suspected of being our friends? Let us unite, then, and
march to glory.

*We swear the most inviolable respect for your properties,
your laws, and all your religious opinions. Be free! be
masters in your own country. We look for no other conquest than that of your liberty—no other success than
yours.*

The moment of breaking your chains has arrived; our tri-
umphant troops are now flying to the extremities of the earth
to tear up the roots of the wealth and tyranny of our enemies.
That frightened Colossus is mouldering away in every part.
Can there be any Irishman base enough to separate himself at
such a happy conjuncture from the grand interests of his
country? If such there be, brave friends, let him be chased
from the country he betrays, and let his property become the
reward of those generous men who know how to fight and
die!

Irishmen, recollect the late defeats which your enemies have
experienced from the French; recollect the claims of Hons-
coote, Toulon, Quiberon, and Ostend; recollect America, free
from the moment she wished to be so.

The contest between you and your oppressors cannot be
long.

Union! Liberty! the *Irish Republic!* such is our shout.
Let us march. Our hearts are devoted to you; our glory is in
your happiness.

HUMBERT.

The forenoon of the 23d was occupied in trans-
porting the munition and military stores from the
ships to the town of Killala. Having attended to
this and placed his prisoners in charge of Savary,
Humbert next bethought himself of the enemy. He

sent Sarrazin—promoted to the rank of general of brigade for his spirited conduct of the preceding day—with a small force in the direction of Ballina to reconnoitre the country. Ballina, a fishing town on the River Moy, was in the hands of several troops of carabineers and yeomanry infantry under the command of Colonel Sir Thomas Chapman and Major Kerr, the greater part of which had come up during the night by forced marches from Foxford—another point still further to the south—on the first alarm of Humbert's arrival. Sarrazin's movements were so rapid and unexpected that he fell upon a party of the enemy engaged in feeding their horses, and almost succeeded in surrounding them. A sharp engagement followed, ending in the flight of the British. After pursuing them two leagues, Sarrazin, considering his mission accomplished, returned in the afternoon to Killala.

Here the preparations for an active campaign were being pushed with great energy. Humbert's programme being to organize a regular army composed of Irishmen, he assembled all the leading agitators of the vicinity, to obtain their aid and counsel. It was at this period, already, that he discovered the great gulf which separated the French Republican and Freethinker from the Irish patriot and Catholic. Humbert, a soldier of the nation that had driven the pope from Italy, found himself, to his surprise, the would-be deliverer of a race to whom the pontiff was but one remove from the

Deity itself. The situation was as startling as it was unexpected, not to him alone but to every one of his followers—sons of the great revolution, worshippers at the shrine of "Liberty" and "Reason," to whom the old religions, one and all, were part and parcel of a system for the enslaving of the human mind and body. From the neck of every one of the sturdy peasants who by hundreds gathered in front of the castle, clamoring for arms and the opportunity to march against the common foe, hung a square piece of brown cloth with the letters I. H. S.[1] inscribed on it. These were scapulars intended to arm them with fresh courage and protect them from danger in the hour of trial. Some carried banners decorated with the embroidered counterfeit of the Virgin Mary and infant Jesus; some held up crucifixes for their companions to adore. All greeted the French as defenders of the true religion, and asked for the confiscation of all Protestant property; and the more bloodthirsty even demanded that the entire extirpation of the heretics be commenced without delay.

To Humbert the situation was embarrassing in the extreme. On the one hand, by rejecting the demands of the insurgents he risked losing their much-needed assistance; on the other, by acceding to them he would be violating the rules of war and exposing himself and his men to the vengeance of the enemy in case of defeat. He called to mind

[1] *Jesus hominum Salvator.*

Moreau's refusal to execute the Directory's bloodthirsty decree, ordering the killing of English and
Hanoverian prisoners of war, and decided to adopt
a similar course. The insurgents were therefore
told in unmistakable terms that all attempts to
harm any loyalist would be met with summary punishment of the offender.

In a grandiloquent manner suited to the necessities of the case, Humbert addressed his hearers,
through the medium of an interpreter, somewhat as
follows: "Citizens and brethren: understand that we
are soldiers, not highway robbers. We have landed
here to fight the armies of the King of England
and save your unfortunate country—not to wage
war on private citizens. We in France acknowledge no religion that preaches intolerance toward
another. We believe as little in your Pope as in
your Established Church—Catholics and Protestants are the same to us. We believe only in justice
and charity to all mankind."

This harangue, short and decisive, produced for
the time being the desired result. Murmurs were
audible for a moment, but the wiser counsel prevailed and the recruiting proceeded without further
hindrance. Strange to say, most active, in a certain sense, in promoting the interests of the French
were the priests themselves, whose mission Humbert had inferentially deprecated. Not so much
that they placed patriotism above religious preju-
dice. To them the bearing of the invaders could

never have been a disappointment, for were they
not fully cognizant of the republic's treatment of
the clergy ?   In their hearts these servants of Rome
detested the Freethinker as cordially as they abomi-
nated their Protestant fellow-citizen; but, imbued
with the Machiavellian spirit of the Church, they
seized with avidity the opportunity of annihilating
one foe through the instrumentality of another.
From beginning to end the influence of several of
their number was insidiously directed toward en-
compassing the suppression if not the total destruction of the " Orangemen," a term indiscriminately
applied to all non-Catholics, and but for the energetic interposition of the French the massacres of
Scullabogue and Wexford [1] would in all probability
have found their counterparts in the province of
Connaught.   That the parish priests especially were
very assiduous at the start in swelling the ranks of
the rebel forces cannot be denied, and their services
were fully appreciated by the French commander,
but he never considered them any the more entitled
to the privilege of maltreating or plundering their
unprotected enemies.   To cite one example, a priest
named Sweeney, who, with a body of his parishion-
ers, had joined the invaders almost immediately after
their arrival, approached Lieutenant-Colonel Charost
with the request that Bishop Stock's library be
made over to him, as he was very fond of books.

---

[1] Two towns of Leinster in which horrible atrocities were committed by the rebels during the outbreak of '98.

"The bishop's library," replied Charost in a tone of contempt, "is just as much his own now as it ever was."[1] Another worthy representative of the Church militant was Father Owen Cowley, of the parish of Castleconnor, Sligo, who, if the affidavits of his victims can be credited, spared no pains to bring about the wholesale slaughter of the English prisoners confined at Ballina. Though he failed in this pious design his treatment of them was cruel in the extreme.

But this phase of the campaign will receive further attention in another chapter. For the present it is only necessary to say that the incongruity of the various elements gathered together in Killala could only be compared to the unprecedented nature of the situation itself. For the first time, perhaps, in the world's history, the passions of warring religionists were restrained by the intervention of neutrals entirely devoid of all religious belief. Still more extraordinary was the fact that many of the latter had but two years before been engaged in deadly strife with an element very similar in most respects to the people they had now come to deliver from bondage. In the bloody struggle of La Vendée the republicans had been opposed to men of Celtic race and intense Catholicism—men abhorring every other form of government save that sanctified by the Holy Father and his servant, the king. Now the position was reversed. The scapu-

[1] *Narrative of What Passed at Killala.*

lar, the Church banner, the censer and the crucifix
were to be paraded side by side with the tricolor of
Atheism and Revolution.   War and politics make
strange bed-fellows, indeed !

MARQUIS OF CORNWALLIS.

CHAPTER IV.

AVING stated the situation of the invading force, let us glance at the field of operations and the dispositions for defence made by the British military authorities. At the conclusion of the first chapter allusion was made to the rebellious outbreaks in counties Wexford and Wicklow and the province of Ulster, during May and June, 1798, and their bloody suppression by the troops of the king. These different disturbances had resulted in the concentration in various portions of the unfortunate country of bodies of regulars and militia aggregating 150,000 men, under the supreme command of Lord Cornwallis, the brave opponent of Washington. The regulars constituted the flower of the English Army,

and before landing in Ireland had seen service in
the Netherlands, in India and elsewhere. The
militia or yeomanry consisted of volunteers recruited from the body of the Protestant population
of the country—descendants of the earlier English
and Scotch invaders and settlers. The corps came
into existence in the autumn of 1796, at the instance of the government, which, foreseeing the evil
consequences likely to ensue from the prevailing
abuses, desired to build up a solid dam against the
inflowing tide of popular indignation. In the teeth
of Catholic opposition a measure passed the Irish
Parliament creating a force of 20,000 men, and this
number swelled to 36,000 before the end of the first
six months. During the rebellion the yeomanry
force exceeded 50,000 men of all arms.

With regard to the discipline and moral standing
of the army as a whole, it is sufficient to quote the
opinion of Sir Ralph Abercromby, who, after short
service, retired from its command as involving, in
his opinion, duties unworthy of a soldier. On February 26, 1798, this gallant officer, in an official report, declared that he had found the force "in such
a state of licentiousness that must render it formidable to every one but the enemy!" Of the yeomanry in particular Lord Cornwallis, on July 8th,
or less than three weeks after his appointment to
the lord-lieutenancy of Ireland, wrote the following
scathing denunciation to Lord Portland:

"The Irish militia are totally without discipline;

contemptible before the enemy when serious resistance is made to them, but ferocious and cruel in the extreme when any poor wretches, either with or without arms, come within their power ; in short, murder appears to be their favorite pastime." Writing to General Ross, the lord-lieutenant furthermore declared that England was engaged " in a war of plunder and massacre ; " and, after referring to court-martial executions, continued : " But all this is trifling compared to the numberless murders that are hourly committed by our people without any process of examination whatever."

No comments of the historian, however unbiassed he be, can carry the weight that attaches to these statements of the two most chivalrous British officers of the day.

The first English commander to receive intelligence of the French landing at Killala was Major-General John Hely Hutchinson, stationed with a large force in the town of Galway. Without awaiting instructions from his superior, the Marquis of Cornwallis, he resolved to march northward with all his available troops, leaving the southern section to take care of itself as best it could, both against a possible rebellion or another French descent. His corps was composed of the Kerry militia, recruited in Galway, some Kilkenny yeomanry from Loughrea, a body of Longford militia from Gort, a detachment of so-called Royal Roxburgh Fencible Dragoons under the command of Lord Roden, several

companies of a Highland regiment known as the
Fraser Fencibles, and four six-pounders and a howitzer served by men of the Royal Irish Artillery.

Almost simultaneously with this movement of
troops from the south occurred a still more formidable one from the west. Lord Cornwallis was
apprised of the invasion on the 24th of August.
With his usual energy he took immediate measures
to meet the emergency, and as a preliminary step
despatched General Gerard Lake to the town of
Galway to conduct the operations commenced from
that point. Then, collecting as many troops as
could be spared in the east, he started in person
for Connaught. He arrived at Phillipstown on the
26th with the One Hundredth Regiment Royal Infantry, the First and Second of Light Infantry, and
the flank companies of the Buck and Warwick militia. Two days later the army had already reached
the village of Kilbeggan, forty-four miles further
west—a fact that speaks well for the endurance of
the troops and the resolution of their commander.

Having completed his arrangements for an offen-
sive movement, Humbert, on the other hand, on the
morning of August 24th left Killala with the major
portion of his army—if, indeed, his handful of men
may be dignified by this term—and struck for the
south. His primary object was to drive the enemy
from Ballina, after which he intended marching on
to Castlebar, the county town of Mayo, where he
had learned that a concentration of troops was con-

templated. He hoped by a march into the interior to enlist every Catholic in the cause of Irish liberty, and thus add to his feeble strength; for, to tell the truth, the results of the two first days' recruiting had been a bitter disappointment to him. A goodly proportion of the raw levies, after realizing that their deliverers were thoroughly determined to prevent the plundering of the Protestants, had simply dropped out of the ranks and settled down at a safe distance to await developments.

Before long the vanguard of the French force espied the British troops posted in an advantageous position a few miles north of Ballina. Major Kerr had received considerable reënforcements, including some veteran cavalry, and had boldly pressed forward to encounter the foe. As on the two previous occasions, Sarrazin led the attack of the French. His detachment consisted of the grenadiers—about two hundred picked men—and one battalion of the line. Dismounting from his horse, he placed himself at the head of the foremost column, and with a theatrical gesture, calculated to impress his men— French soldiers have ever been impressed by trifles —ordered the advance at double-quick. "*À la baïonette*" was his battle-cry, and it reëchoed all along the line; and the blue-coated troopers sprang with their wonted agility over the broken ground and threw themselves against the front ranks of the enemy with an irresistible *élan*. Still, Major Kerr was not unprepared for the attack, and the rapid

5

but regular platoon firing of the yeomanry and carabineers might have proved an effectual check even
to the veteran grenadiers had not General-Adjutant
Fontaine turned the flank of the British position,
and poured in his volleys almost on their rear. Seeing himself in danger of being surrounded, Major
Kerr sounded the retreat, which became a disorderly rout when Humbert appeared in person with
a detachment of the third regiment of Chasseurs
mounted on horses obtained in Killala.[1]

[1] The author of this sketch considers it incumbent upon him to
point out that very serious discrepancies exist in the different accounts of these preliminary military operations following upon the
landing of the French. Humbert, for instance, in his report to the
Directory, distinctly refers to two skirmishes having occurred north
of Ballina, one on the 6th Fructidor (23d of August), and the other
on the following day, as narrated above.

Fontaine, on the other hand, speaks of three different engagements as having taken place between the capture of Killala and the
final occupation of Ballina. The first fight was the result of a reconnoissance undertaken by General Sarrazin and Captain Huet and a
body of grenadiers. The enemy was " four hundred strong and was
easily dispersed." The second engagement occurred on the 7th
Fructidor (August 24th), and its details as given by Fontaine tally
with Humbert's report. The third engagement took place on the
morning of the 25th under the walls of Ballina, the British numbering " 1,300 infantry and 700 cavalry !" This last affair is evidently
a product of the writer's vivid imagination.

According to Bishop Stock's account, there was but one engagement, which he describes as follows : He (Humbert) sent on the
next morning (August 23d) toward Ballina a detachment, which, retreating from some piquet guards or reconnoitring parties of loyalists, led them to a bridge under which lay concealed a sergeant's
guard of French soldiers. By a volley from these, a clergyman who

The town of Ballina presented a scene of unutterable confusion when the defeated troops arrived there, all begrimed and gory. The inhabitants of both persuasions sought refuge in their homes, the Catholics from fear of the fugitives, the Protestants from fear of the French. One luckless individual by the name of Walsh, who had previously been arrested on suspicion of disloyalty, but discharged for lack of evidence, was caught in the act of inciting his fellow-citizens to rebellion. Brought before Major Kerr, a commission was found in his pockets, signed by Humbert, authorizing him to gather recruits for the Irish Republic. Without a trial of any kind he was taken to a crane in the market-place and unceremoniously strung up amid the hooting of the *soldateska* and the piteous appeals of his friends.[1] This was the first of a long series of acts of reprisal committed by the king's troops on the unfortunate rebels of Connaught. It was no new pastime to the former. Their hands had already been deeply steeped in the blood of Irish

had volunteered on the occasion and two carabineers were wounded, the first mortally. The clergyman was the Rev. George Fortescue, rector of Ballina. The French, advancing to this town, took possession of it in the night, the garrison retreating to Foxford, leaving one prisoner, a yeoman, in the hands of the enemy.

In view of these discrepancies, the author has deemed it best to accept Humbert's official report as the correct version, and the more so as it is corroborated in the main by Sir Richard Musgrave, the Tory authority.

[1] Musgrave's *Memoirs*, page 577, and *Jones' Narrative*, page 289.

insurgents in Wexford, Ulster and elsewhere. They had grown callous to the dictates of humanity.

The immediate consequences of the second engagement north of Ballina were the evacuation of this town by the royal troops, and the accession to the French ranks of another small corps of Irish recruits. Humbert's field force thus amounted to something over 800 Frenchmen and 1,000 or 1,500 native auxiliaries. The balance of the invading army, numbering 200 rank and file and five officers, under command of Lieutenant-Colonel Charost, had been left in Killala for different reasons. They were needed there to guard a large quantity of ammunition landed by the squadron the day preceding its departure for France,[1] and also to assure the safety of the Protestant population, daily threatened by the more desperate of the United Irishmen. Further, it was feared that an English force from Sligo might attempt a landing at Killala for the purpose of cutting off Humbert's communications, unless the town were adequately protected by a disciplined body of troops. Humbert did not resume his march until the 25th. At three o'clock in the afternoon he moved toward the village of Rappa,[2] and remained there until two in the morning, the delay being caused principally by

[1] Savary, in his letter to the Minister of Marine a month later, declared his sudden departure from Killala to have been caused by a fear of impending tempestuous weather.

[2] Humbert's *Official Reports to the Directory*, dated from Castlebar.

"Sarrazin, by a happy inspiration, stepped up to the crane, threw his arms around the inanimate form, and imprinted a kiss on the livid brow."

—Page 69.

the difficulties in dealing with his new allies, who, as previously stated, lacked every kind of military training.

Sarrazin in the mean time had followed close upon the heels of the retreating British. On the afternoon of the skirmish with Kerr, with drawn sabre, at the head of his grenadiers and chasseurs, he entered the deserted streets of Ballina. As they neared the market square the outlines of a suspended figure became discernible against the white background of a whitewashed building. It was the body of the unfortunate Walsh. When the entire column came up and the identity of the dead man was established, Sarrazin, by a happy inspiration, stepped up to the crane, threw his arms around the inanimate form, and imprinted a kiss on the livid brow. " *Voilà, Messieurs,*" he cried, turning to the Irish auxiliaries, " thus do we honor the martyrs of your sacred cause." Major O'Keon translated the words into the native vernacular, and the assemblage, now swelled by two-thirds of the town's inhabitants, joined in a deafening shout of applause. Each company, in passing the swaying body, dipped its colors and presented arms, and, each in his turn, the different commanders stepped up to the corpse and gave it the embrace of " sympathetic civism." Had the entire comedy been prearranged instead of being a clever impromptu, it could not have passed off more propitiously, or made so deep an impression on the spectators.

The experiences of the last few days had taught
the French that the deeply rooted religious sentiments of the native Irish must be respected, and
with that faculty for adapting themselves to circumstances which seems to be inherent in the Gaul, the
invaders decided to turn these very sentiments to
the best possible account. Accordingly, after indulging in the little scene just described, Sarrazin
ordered Walsh's body to be cut down and carried to
the nearest Romish chapel. Here it was attired in
a French military suit, placed in a handsome coffin
and laid out in state, surrounded by burning tapers
and mourners with crucifixes and censers. And all
this to the tune of the " Marseillaise " and "Ça
Ira," and the sacriligious jests—fortunately not un-
derstood by those at whom they were directed—of
the French Republican soldiery !

The French did not stop here in their efforts to
conciliate the Catholic element. They were playing
a desperate game, and appreciating that everything
was at stake, they hesitated at no measure, short of
compliance with the demanded persecution of the
Protestants, that would insure the most efficient aid
from that source. Acting under instructions from
the commander-in-chief, O'Keon mounted a ros-
trum in the market-place of Ballina and told the
assembled throng the following interesting story in
Irish : He dreamt one night, he said, that the Holy
Mother of God visited his bedside and poured into
his ear the story of Ireland's suffering and woe.

This done, she called upon him to arise, return home, and battle in the cause of Irish freedom. The speaker declared that he at first regarded the apparition as an idle dream, unworthy of serious consideration; but a few nights later the visit was repeated. This time she bemoaned in still more melancholic accents the condition of his mother country, and urged him once more to return home. Still taking no notice of the warning, the speaker received a third visit, his heavenly guest making herself felt, as well as heard, by administering a sharp box on his ear. Convinced by this manifestation that the Madonna's order was seriously meant, O'Keon repaired to the French Directory and persuaded them to undertake this expedition! He assured his hearers that the success of the enterprise must be a foregone conclusion, as the Holy Mother had herself advised it and would never abandon her faithful followers.[1] O'Keon's harangue was received with every demonstration of delight by the impressionable peasantry, not one of whom appeared to doubt a single word of it.

Humbert entered Ballina early on Sunday, the 26th, with the main body, but his stay there was very short. Peasants came in during the morning with the information that the enemy's forces at Castlebar were hourly increasing. General Hutchinson had arrived there, they said, with his Galway division, and reënforcements were constantly join-

[1] Musgrave's *Memoirs,* page 583.

ing him.[1]   This was, therefore, no time for dilly-
dallying.   After a few hours' rest the French general, with his entire corps, moved out of Ballina
toward the capital of Mayo.   It was three o'clock
in the afternoon, and threatening clouds were gathering on the horizon.   The heavens, the landscape,
and the prospects of the marching hundreds seemed
equally gloomy.

[1] These reënforcements comprised the troops mentioned by Cornwallis in his letter of August 25th to the Duke of Portland. '' Several regiments," he wrote, '' were moving from the southeast part of
the island toward Connaught before we heard of the landing of the
French."

" The heavens, the landscape, and the prospects of the marching hundreds, seemed equally gloomy."
—Page 72.

CHAPTER V.

UMBERT'S theatre of operations belonged to one of the most picturesque portions of Ireland. A remote corner of the country, little visited by outsiders, its rugged aspect had remained unchanged for centuries. Its physical formation was most varied in nature: rocky heights and precipitous cliffs, covered with brush and heather, alternating with verdant plains, upon which browsed well-fed cattle. The banks of the River Moy, which empties its waters into the Bay of Killala, had been the scene of many an episode in early Irish history, and traces of a greater past were visible on all sides. The romantic ruins of Rosskerk, Belleck and Moyne abbeys—the theme of many a poet's song—lying between Killala and Ballina,

attested to the artistic and architectural glories of
a generation unfettered by the chains of the conqueror. In short, nature and history had combined
to add to the poetry impregnating the very air of
this most thoroughly Celtic section of the Green
Isle.

There are two roads leading from Ballina to Castlebar. One almost skirts the River Moy to the
town of Foxford, after which it turns to the south-
west. This was the usual route chosen by travel-
lers. The other one branches from Ballina in a
westerly direction, winding around Lough Conn, a
lake noted for the majestic beauty of its rocky
banks. At the town of Crossmalina the road turns
abruptly southward and crosses the mountains of
Fanogue. It passes under the shadow of the great
Nephin, an imposing mountain over 2,000 feet high,
and at a point called Barnageehy becomes a narrow
defile that, properly defended, could defy the assaults of another Xerxes. About fifteen miles in a
direct line south of Crossmalina lies Castlebar, in a
plain near a large lough. The capital of the county,
it is the point of convergence of numerous roads
and highways. A small river flows by the town,
and is crossed by a stone bridge of ancient construction. The name of Castlebar is derived from
a fortress of the De Burgh family, long since a ruin.
Sir Henry Bingham held the castle for Parliament
in the old Cromwellian days, and, besieged by Lord
Mayo in 1641, he surrendered it on favorable condi-

tions. These, however, were treacherously violated, and he and the entire garrison were put to the sword. Mayo's treachery was avenged twelve years later on his son, Sir Theodore Burke, who suffered death at the headsman's hands. At the time of our narrative Castlebar was a fairly prosperous city of about 3,000 inhabitants, exclusive of the military. It possessed a strong stone jail, a court-house, and the usual county offices, situated in a square in the centre of the town. Its long main thoroughfare was intersected by smaller and narrower ones, eminently adapted to street warfare.

The English army from Galway, under Major-Generals Hutchinson and Trench, reached Castlebar late at night on the 24th of August. At the same time Brigadier-General Robert Taylor, commandant of the garrison of Sligo, had approached from the northeast with a considerable force. When he entered Foxford he found written orders from Hutchinson directing him to remain there and await the French, who were expected to select that route in preference to the one by Barnageehy. In spite of Hutchinson's executive ability and his popularity among his men, so great had become the demoralization of the army that preparations for encountering the invaders were attended with the greatest difficulty. Fights and broils between the regulars and the militia were of hourly occurrence, and even indulgence in intoxicating liquors seems

to have been not infrequent. The disgraceful
scenes reached their climax on Sunday night, the
26th, after the main body of the Longford militia
had entered town. The men were bivouacked on
the green, eating bread and cheese, when a shot,
discharged from a window close by, fell in their
midst. Immediately a stupendous uproar ensued.
" In the dark of the night," wrote an eye-witness,
" four thousand enraged soldiers in the town!
A noise arose—the clamor of irritated passions.
Arms clashed against each other, and glass flew
from windows, whilst the enraged men called for
vengeance on the culprit. The general shouted for
the officer commanding (Captain Chambers) to
stand in the street until the affair should be over.
The fellow who fired the shot fled off when he
thought he had kindled a flame which would
destroy the town. I am told if there had not
been instant peace the general would have caused
the cannon to be brought to bear on the street
and swept it with grapeshot; but glory to the
Prince of Peace! he gave us a silent street in ten
minutes." [1]

The writer of the above was an old inhabitant of
Castlebar, who, being thoroughly well acquainted
with the surrounding country, drew out a detailed
map thereof on the night of the 26th, and sent it to
General Hutchinson. His guest on this occasion
was Captain Chambers, one of the few real heroes

[1] *Jones' Narrative,* page 290.

of the royal army. As an illustration of the piet-
istic spirit prevailing among Protestants in those
days, it may not be uninteresting to quote the following anecdote from the same authority :

"A little before day (August 27)," he says, "my
wife told me : 'I will see the battle in the street,
having in a dream beheld flags—a green, and
another of a different color.' We then agreed to
consult the Bible. I first opened for our army,
2 Kings, vii. 7 : 'Wherefore they arose and fled in
the twilight, and left their tents, and their houses,
even the camp as it was, and fled for their life.'
We next opened for our country, Jer. v. 15 : 'Lo, I
will bring a nation upon you from afar, O house of
Israel, saith the Lord ; it is a mighty nation, it is an
ancient nation, a nation whose language thou knowest not, neither understandest what they say.' I
next opened for our king, Psalms, lxi. 7 : ' He shall
abide before God forever: O prepare mercy and
truth which may preserve him.' I lastly opened
for my wife and myself, John, xiii. 7 : ' Jesus
answered and said unto him : ' What I do thou
knowest not now, but thou shalt know hereafter.'
From all these I concluded that we should lose *that*
battle, but that the king and constitution would
still be upheld."

Unfortunately for the arms of England, General
Hutchinson was not destined to lead the king's
troops in the coming struggle. On Saturday night,
between ten and eleven o'clock, General Lake, the

ruthless exterminator of thousands of patriots in
the county of Wexford, rode into Castlebar with
his staff and took command of the army. Almost
from the moment of his arrival disagreements
arose between him and Hutchinson.[1] The latter,
though suffering from a severe attack of fever, had
taken pains to study the topography of the surroundings, and had inspected every inch of ground
within a radius of many miles, the result being a
very efficient and comprehensive plan of operations, which, if carried out, say the apologists of
the English, would have effectually disposed of
Humbert and his weak force. Lake, however, belonged to that class of Englishmen, unfortunately
very large, who entertain a supreme contempt for
foreigners of every description, among others for
the French. He had been brought up from boy-
hood to believe that one English soldier was a
match for at least two Frenchmen, three Spaniards,
four Dutchmen, and an inconceivable number of
savages—a pleasant delusion that even his partici-
pation in the inglorious campaigns in the Netherlands against revolutionary France does not seem
to have materially affected. He was a tried soldier,
however, having entered the army at the age of
fourteen, and had won laurels during the Seven
Years' War in Germany, and under Cornwallis in
America. Martinet and Tory, he detested all rebels
from the bottom of his heart. Hence his selection

[1] Reverend J. Gordon's *History of the Rebellion.*

by the British Ministry to succeed the mild and humane Abercromby. In suppressing the uprising in Wexford, he had not failed to give vent to his passionate hatred of revolution in any form, as the thousands of desolated homes and orphaned families fully attested.

When news arrived at the British headquarters at Castlebar that Humbert's army, on the march from Ballina, exclusive of the Irish corps, fell short of eight hundred regulars, Lake thrust aside Hutchinson's maps and plans with a gesture of disdain. Lord Jocelin's " Fox Hunters," he declared, would suffice to account for so insignificant a foe, even if Taylor failed to hold his own at Foxford. The " Fox Hunters" were a body of light horse attached to Lake's cavalry, who had distinguished themselves at the Curragh of Kildare, a short time before, by treacherously butchering in cold blood a division of rebel prisoners. The unfortunates had surrendered on the express stipulation that their lives should be spared.

During all this time General Humbert's army was slowly but steadily plodding on its way to Castlebar. The French general had been informed by one Father Conroy, the parish priest of Adergool, of the Barnageehy route, and had resolved to follow it in preference to the one by Foxford. But in order to deceive the British he first marched his army some distance down the Foxford road, and then at nightfall suddenly turned to his right and

proceeded toward Crossmalina. Father Conroy
rendered another important service to Humbert.
Learning that a man named William Burke had
been despatched to the British commander with
information as to the route of the French, he over-
took the messenger and made him retrace his steps
and take the United Irishmen's oath. Both Conroy
and Burke were afterward hanged at Castlebar by
sentence of an English court-martial.

Many were the hardships of the army during its
tramp over the Fanogue Mountains. Heavy rains
had made the roads almost impassable, and when
the men were not stumbling over rocks or into
crevices they found themselves up to their knees
in incipient bogs. The two curricle guns and the
ammunition wagons, drawn by farm horses, proved
a serious obstacle to the advance, for they were
constantly sticking in the mud. In fact, the poor
beasts soon became entirely unserviceable, and had
to be replaced by the Irish peasantry, who performed the tedious task with cheerfulness. The
carriage of one of the guns broke down, and its
repairing delayed the army a couple of hours. Yet
no signs of faltering were visible on the counte-
nances of the weary but determined men. The
French had surmounted greater difficulties than
these in their former campaigns, and had never
known defeat. They hummed snatches of patriotic
songs to keep up their spirits, and exchanged com-
pliments with the Irish contingent, some of whom

aroused no little good-natured mirth by their awkward movements and unsuccessful attempts to assume a martial bearing. Not an incident occurred during the whole march to ruffle the harmonious relations of the allies, so different in sentiments and temperament.

With the dawn of day the column emerged from the pass of Barnageehy and descended into the vale beyond. A Protestant yeoman, who was visiting his farm in the vicinity, saw a line of blue coats in the distance, and dismayed beyond measure, sped to Castlebar with the intelligence. His story obtained no credence, so convinced were the British commanders that Humbert had chosen the Foxford route; but to make entirely sure, General Trench set out in person to reconnoitre, attended by a few dragoons. The party rode three miles in a northerly direction, when they were fired upon by a French picket. There was no doubt about it now. The French *were* coming, and at a rapid pace, too! The horsemen whipped up their steeds and galloped back to Castlebar, with feelings akin to those experienced by the yeoman.

In a few moments after their arrival the stillness of the morn was broken by the sound of alarm bells, the bugle's blast, and the shouts and vociferations of the excited soldiery. Realizing the gravity of the situation and his own helplessness, General Lake gave Hutchinson *carte blanche* to arrange the troops in line of battle. Hutchinson at once sent

6

orderlies to the various division commanders with
instructions to march to an elevation at the northeast extremity of the town, known as Mount Bur-
ren, which had been selected the day before as an
alarm post. A good deal of confusion resulted
from the unexpectedness of the alarm, but within
an hour some order was restored, and when the sun
burst out from over the hillocks on the east the
British army, about 6,000 strong, with 18 guns, was
drawn up in an imposing battle array, prepared to
receive the enemy.

It is well to state that this calculation as to the
strength of the English at Castlebar is based on the
most reliable authority. It is true that General
Hutchinson, in an official statement submitted to
Lord Cornwallis a month later,[1] placed the numbers of the loyalists at " 1,600, or 1,700 cavalry and
infantry, 10 pieces of cannon and one howitzer,"
and his testimony is evidently accepted as unim-
peachable by Mr. Froude and the few other British
historians who have deigned to notice the affair of
August 27th, 1798. But if any credence can be
placed in Sir Richard Musgrave's account of the
battle—and it is certainly the most detailed in existence—Hutchinson's estimate falls very far short
of the truth. Musgrave, as a loyalist, carefully
avoids mentioning figures altogether; but as he
gives a list of the various infantry regiments pres-

[1] This statement is included in the *Correspondence of the Marquis
of Cornwallis.*

ent on the field, it is comparatively easy to approx-
imate their numerical strength, which by the lowest calculation must have aggregated 5,000 men.
Francis Plowden, another writer of the day, also a
loyalist, but one of a far different calibre to Musgrave in breadth of mind, declares Lake's army to
have "fallen little short of 6,000 men," including
the cavalry, an assertion supported by many actors
in the short and bloody drama.[1]

" The sudden progress of such a handful of men
into the very centre of the island," wrote a yeoman
in Lake's army to his brother in Castlebar, "was, I
think, a clear comment on the words of Solomon,
that ' the race is not to the swift nor the battle to
the strong.' Thus what 6,000 men could not do at
Castlebar five flank companies and a few cavalry
effected at Ballinamuck."[2] Equally reliable testimony in the same direction is furnished by Bishop
Stock, who says : " The enemy's main body had
hardly marched from Killala when a flag of truce
arrived from Castlebar, carried by Captain Grey, of
the Carabineers. It came under the pretence of in-

---

[1] Here is what Plowden incidentally remarks : " It must ever remain an humiliating reflection upon the lustre and power of the
British arms that so pitiful a detachment as that of 1,100 French infantry should, in a kingdom in which there was an armed force of
above 150,000 men, have not only put to rout a select army of 6,000
men prepared to receive the invaders, but also provided themselves
with ordnance and ammunition from our stores, taken several of our
towns," etc.

[2] *Jones' Narrative*, page 326.

quiry after an officer who was wounded and made
prisoner at Ballina, but the object of it was to learn
the force of the enemy. As soon as this was
known, Captain Grey privately desired us not to be
uneasy, for a force equal to three times their number was waiting at Castlebar to give a good account
of them." Captain (or lieutenant) Grey returned to
Castlebar on Saturday,[1] the 25th—that is, long before the last reënforcement reached that town.

To reduce the matter to a few words, Humbert's
army of 800 men—the Irish contingent for reasons
shortly to be stated need not be included—found
itself opposed to a force almost eight times its
superior in size.

That General Hutchinson, whose conduct throughout the engagement was beyond all praise, should
have rendered himself guilty of wilful misrepre-
sentation, is only excusable on the ground perhaps
that he considered himself justified as an officer of
his Majesty in shielding the reputation of the British
arms. No such duty devolves on the British historian, who in this case, however, has only followed
his time-honored custom of pandering to the inor-
dinate national vanity of his countrymen. The
average Englishman goes through life with an
exalted conviction of Britannia's superiority over
all other nations. Not content with her unques-
tioned supremacy on the sea and in the world of
commerce, he would wish her military record to

[1] General Hutchinson's statement, Sept. 21, 1798.

GENERAL JOHN HELY HUTCHINSON.

dazzle the eyes of all creation. So firm a hold has this hobby gained upon him that paltry skirmishes figure in English history as important battles, and mediocre captains are magnified into Cæsars and Alexanders. Maida[1] is mentioned in the same breath with Austerlitz, and Wellington, who never risked an engagement save when the chances were overwhelmingly in his favor, is ranked above the great Napoleon. The same tone of empty and arrogant boasting pervades alike the pages of most English historical works and the utterances of the large class of British " Jingoes." But this vanity were a bagatelle if the truth were not constantly sacrificed on its altar. Chauvinism and mendacity flourish in the same soil !

The British at Castlebar were drawn up in three lines running from east to west across the crest of the hill. They commanded a slight elevation in front, over which any attacking force from the north must necessarily pass. The first line consisted of a portion of the artillery, including two curricle guns served by men of the Royal Irish Artillery under Captain Shortall, an experienced officer, the Kilkenny Militia, a portion of the 6th Regiment of Foot under Major McBean, and a detachment of the Prince of Wales' Fencibles. Captain Shortall himself took post with the two curricle guns in front of the line, the Kilkenny regiment being stationed

[1] An insignificant and indecisive skirmish fought July 4, 1806, in Calabria. It figures as a great victory in English history.

at his right and the Kilkenny artillery to his left,
separated by a road, but parallel to him. The second line was composed of what might be called the
flower of the army, the Fraser Fencibles—Scotch
Highlanders in their national tartans, plaids, and
feathers, who had fought bravely throughout the
rebellion without dimming the lustre of their arms
by acts of wanton cruelty. The Frasers were supported by a corps of Galway militiamen, both bodies having been drawn up in irregular lines so as to
fully occupy the summits of the British position.
In a valley on the left of the elevation held by the
Kilkenny troops stood several companies of Longford yeomanry.

However, the strength of Lake's army lay principally in its cavalry, which comprised some of
the best troops in the king's service. There
was " Lord Jocelin's Light Horse," already mentioned for their treacherous cruelty in Kildare;
there was the 6th Carabineers; the 23d Light Dragoons; Lord Roden's Roxborough Fencible Cavalry, and several squadrons of yeomanry horse.[1]
The bulk of this imposing body of mounted men
occupied a large space in the rear of the first line,
Lake's apparent intention being to throw them
upon the foe as soon as the artillery and musketry
fire had sown confusion in his ranks. Among
the officers commanding the king's forces were
a number of English and Anglo-Irish noblemen

[1] C. H. Teeling's *Personal Narrative*, p. 216.

who had promised themselves good sport shooting down the *Sans-culottes* and hanging the "croppies."[1] It never occurred to them that, with a tremendous numerical superiority in favor of the British, the choice of position, and an enemy exhausted by fifteen hours' steady marching, any other result could be possible!

When, toward eight o'clock, General Humbert and his staff arrived within sight of the British lines and beheld the heights scarlet with the uniforms of the regulars and militia, they concluded within themselves that the game was lost in advance. At a glance they recognized the fact that the one possibility they had counted on, *viz.*, a surprise of the enemy, was out of the question. Nothing now remained to counterbalance his weight of numbers and his almost unassailable front. Humbert decided that if he were destined to succumb he would at least maintain the honor of his flag. He accordingly took immediate measures to attack the British position. He first formed a column from the ranks of the Irish insurgents, and sent them ahead to drive in the English outposts and commence the assault on the foremost line of artillery. Close behind the Irish followed General Sarrazin with the Grenadiers. Short work was made of the outposts, and elated by their easy success the simple-minded peasants,

[1] "Croppy" was a term of opprobrium applied by the king's troops to the rebels. It originated from the fact that the latter wore their hair cropped close to their heads.

many of them clad in the French uniform, made a
bold dash at the enemy's guns. Not a sound issued
from these until the assailants were within fifty
yards. Then Captain Shortall gave the signal, the
gunners applied their fuses, and the head of the
attacking column was literally split in twain, the
messengers of destruction leaving a furrow thickly
strewn with dead and dying. The survivors—most
of whom in their unfrequented regions had never,
perhaps, until that day heard the report of a musket,
much less witnessed the effects of artillery fire—
were overwhelmed with terror. They turned upon
their heels and sped down the mountain side in
wild confusion. They took no further share in the
battle of Castlebar.

It was now the turn of the French to face
Shortall's fire. Sarrazin's Grenadiers, undisturbed
by the precipitate flight of their allies, marched
steadily up the slope with fixed bayonets, and
approached the British centre. At the same time a
battalion of the line moved toward the British left.
The French were aided in their movements by the
peculiar formation of the ground, which, intersected
by stone walls and high hedges, afforded them
excellent shelter against the small-arms' fire of the
enemy. Sarrazin's first attack, however, proved a
failure. The English artillery, superbly served,
once more performed its deadly office. One of
Shortall's shots cut clean through the infantry
battalion, who, seeing themselves taken at a disad-

vantage, ran to the cover of a small house near by. The Grenadiers then wheeled half way, and under a galling musketry and artillery fire rushed to the relief of their brethren. After this the attacking force retreated down the slope, leaving many dead and wounded. A very brief period intervened before the next attack. The French this time attempted to neutralize the effects of the enemy's marksmanship by driving some cattle in front of them, but such of the poor brutes as were not shot down at the first discharge scampered, terror-stricken, into the very ranks they were intended to screen, nearly causing irremediable disorder.

So far the tide of fortune had been against the assailants, yet from this very circumstance there gleamed for Humbert a ray of hope. The inertness of the British, and their neglect to follow up their advantages, satisfied him that they were badly led. The moment had therefore arrived to hazard a bold stroke—no less than a general attack along the whole length of the enemy's line! To do this it became necessary to extend the French front until it should overlap his left wing. At the word of command the sturdy little Frenchmen deployed from the centre with the rapidity and precision of a dress-parade, and when they commenced their next advance up the steep incline the British looked down in amazement on a long, thin line of blue in open order, its full strength not exceeding five hundred bayonets! Was this skeleton force about to brave the entire British front ?   Such audacity was scarcely conceivable.[1]

It was a critical moment.   A combined effort of the English would probably have given the day to them.   As it was, the infantry supporting the guns seemed to have lost their heads.   Instead of await-ing their foe at close quarters they commenced firing in a desultory fashion at so great a distance as to produce no effect.   Orders of any kind from the commanding general were lacking, and the splendid cavalry corps stood inactive within its lines.   Only the Highlanders posted behind a fringe of bushes on the British left and the artillery ap-peared to understand their duty, and to perform it.

[1] Contemporaneous descriptions of the physique and *morale* of the contending forces form an interesting contrast.   Of the French, Bishop Stock says : " Intelligence, activity, temperance, patience, to a surprising degree, appeared to be combined in the soldiery that came over with Humbert, together with the exactest obedience to discipline ; yet, if you except the Grenadiers, they had nothing to catch the eye.   Their stature for the most part was low, their com-plexion pale and sallow, their clothes much the worse for wear ; to a superficial observer they would have appeared incapable of enduring almost any hardship.   These were the men, however, of whom it was presently observed that they could be well content to live on bread or potatoes, to drink water, to make the stones of the street their bed, and to sleep in their clothes with no cover but the canopy of heaven."

Speaking of Lake's men, the Under Secretary for Ireland, in his letter to William Wickham, Aug. 31, 1798, remarks that they are " fine regiments in appearance, fine men and well drilled, capable in point of body, youth and agility, and *habilité* to face any troops." *Correspondence of the Marquis of Cornwallis*, page 393.

Perceiving the lack of cohesion among the British, Sarrazin ordered the *Pas de charge* sounded,
and the French rushed forward to some hedges
immediately in the enemy's front. Under cover
of these they continued to advance in separate
bodies, uttering the while their war cries and
firing as rapidly as they could reload. As they
came nearer some confusion was perceptible in
the English ranks. The artillery was vomiting
grape and canister, but the fire of the infantry had
slackened. Now that the soldiers of the republic
were at hand with their deadly bayonets, the war-
riors of his Majesty felt their hearts fail within
them. Some one raised the cry that the French
were on the flanks, and of a sudden the entire
British infantry—regulars, yeomen and Fencibles—
wavered, broke and beat a hasty retreat, leaving
on the field Major Alcock, sorely wounded, and
many others dead and dying. Sarrazin's men engaged the artillery on the right of the enemy's position, while Chief of Battalion Ardouin attacked the
Frasers and the Galway men on the left. Shortall
had already lost his best soldiers, but instead of
retiring he pulled up his sleeves and took a stand
at one of the guns himself. A French officer
rushed toward him with levelled weapon, and missing fire, drew his sword. The intrepid Englishman,
like many of his compatriots an adept at the manly
art of boxing, doubled up his fists and knocked his
opponent down. He then mounted his horse and

rode away with the same cool and deliberate air
that had signallized his deportment throughout the
engagement.

The astonishing behavior of the infantry on the
British right, and the capture of Shortall's guns, so
alarmed General Lake that he hurriedly ordered
a retreat, and that in the teeth of Hutchinson's
opposition.[1]   The command was superfluous.   The
British formation was already a confused   mass.
Infantry, artillery and cavalry, seized with an inde-
scribable panic, were scurrying to the rear, unheed-
ing the exhortations of their officers.   The cavalrymen, gorgeous in scarlet, gold and pipe-clay, with
powdered wigs and clean-shaven faces—the pride of
many a review—presented now a sorry aspect as
they spurred their horses in a mad flight for safety.
Killing prisoners in cold blood was one thing, and
meeting a disciplined foe another!   The former
occupation had unfitted them for the latter.   So
they dashed onward, a disordered horde, riding
down all who crossed their path, whether friend or
foe.   Of the infantry the Longford and Kilkenny
regiments were the most demoralized.   They, too,
had revelled in the blood of their unfortunate compatriots, and as cruelty and cowardice are twin
sisters, fear lent wings to their feet as they fled
from the scene of action.   The Earls of Longford
and Ormond, their respective commanders, vainly
endeavored to rally them.   They were only drawn

[1] Reverend J. Gordon's *History of the Rebellion*, page 285.

into the current themselves. Ormond, chief of the historic Butlers of Ireland, young, handsome and brave, a *preux chevalier* from head to foot, threw himself among his men, in a frenzy of mortification and despair. He implored them impassionately to turn and face the foe. Finding they heeded him not he lost all self-control, and with curses and imprecations laid about him with his sword. He ran two men through the body and left the field with tears of anger streaming down his cheeks. Even when rallied in a churchyard, with a thick wall to protect them, the militia refused to make a stand. The first appearance of the French caused them to scamper over the tombstones like frightened sheep and make their way out by the rear entrance.[1]

At the bridge over the Castlebar River a horrible crush ensued. The main body of the British army had converged to that point, and the narrow structure was blocked with field guns, *caissons* and supply wagons, against which the struggling mass of humanity surged in unreasoning terror. Here it was every one for himself, the alternative to the luckless foot soldier being death under the hoof or a plunge into the waters beneath. To increase the confusion some shots fell in among the fugitives, and in their desperation they turned their weapons against each other. How many perished on the bridge has never been fully ascertained, but for weeks afterward the river and the lough near by

[1] *Correspondence of the Marquis of Cornwallis*, page 393.

threw up mutilated corpses in the uniform of the British line and of the Anglo-Irish yeomanry.

But the battle was not yet over. The most desperate fighting was still to come. By the exertions of the Earl of Granard, Major Thompson, and Captains Chambers and Armstrong, a comparatively large body of men were gotten together to cover the retreat of the army. This they endeavored to do by maintaining a musketry fire from behind hedges and thickets on the approaching *Sans-culottes.* Unable to hold their ground they retired to the bridge, and took up a position there with a curricle gun. At the same moment the Highlanders and some carabineers, after being driven from the left wing at the point of the bayonet, stationed themselves in the public square of Castlebar, where Lieutenant Blundell with two curricle guns had been posted early in the morning. To dislodge the enemy from both these positions, Humbert detached his cavalry from his centre and moved it on to the town, with some infantry under Sarrazin and Adjutant-General Fontaine.

A Protestant citizen present at the battle thus relates some of the details of this conflict: "Colonel Miller," he says, "rushed into the town crying: 'Clear the street for action!' when in a moment, as a dam bursting its banks, a mixture of soldiers of all kinds rushed in at every avenue; a sergeant desired that every woman should go to the barracks; but Dr. Hennin's, another family and mine retired into a house, fell on our knees, and there remained in prayer until the town was taken. . . . Four brave Highlanders at a cannon kept up a brisk fire on the French, but were killed while loading, the gunner taken, and the guns turned on our men. Now the street action became hot; before it was peal answering peal, but now thunder answering thunder; a black cloud of horrors hid the light of heaven—the messengers of death groping their way, as in gloomy hell, whilst the trembling echoes which shook our town concealed the more melancholy groans of the dying. When the French approached the new jail, our sentinel (a Fraser Fencible) killed one Frenchman, charged and killed another, shot a third and a fourth, and, as he fired at and killed the fifth, a number rushed up the steps, dashed his brains out, tumbling him from his stand, and the sentry-box on his body."

The street action lasted nearly an hour, during which period every foot of ground was obstinately disputed. The British, still having the advantage of position and numbers, inflicted severe losses on their opponents, and were only overcome in the end by sheer pluck and hard fighting on the part of the latter. Death had no terrors for these sons of the republic, even though to them it meant not an awakening in another and better world, but chaos and an end of all things. Utterly regardless of grape and canister, of sword and shell, they flung themselves upon the foe. One grenadier, after sabring two gunners, placed his thumb on the touch-hole of a cannon in time to extinguish the burning fuse. He earned his epaulettes for the bold deed, which saved the head of the advancing column from certain destruction.[1] Here and there the town's defenders succeeded in barricading themselves within private dwellings, whence they maintained a galling fire through shutters and improvised loopholes of every description, thus necessitating a series of separate assaults, in which the bayonet played as active a rôle as the bullet.

When the main portion of the town was in their hands the French turned their attention to the bridge. There, as has been mentioned, a body of British with a curricle gun had taken stand. A desperate *melée* was the result. Worked up to a pitch of fury by the bitterness of the preceding conflict, neither side gave nor demanded quarter. The defenders of the bridge consisted of the remnants of many of the regiments present on the field an hour before. There were some Longford and Kilkenny men, a sprinkling of " Frasers," and a corporal's guard or so of the 6th Regiment. The gun itself was worked by the few remaining survivors of Captain Shortall's Royal Irish Artillery Corps. The French began by installing themselves in the deserted buildings near the river's banks, and from here and the roads leading to the bridge they poured volley after volley on the enemy. As soon

---

[1] Fontaine's *Notice Historique*, page 17.

as the last gunner had fallen a squadron of French horse, emerging from the cover of a neighboring house, dashed at the gun, hoping to reach and spike it before assistance arrived. In this they were foiled by the energy of the British officers in command ; but in the hand-to-hand combat that followed fully half of the bridge's defenders were mercilessly cut down. The Chasseurs lost two of their men and drew back ; then, reënforced by the arrival of the infantry, they charged once more and swept the enemy from the field.

Acts of heroism were not lacking during the obstinate struggle. Captain Chambers, on the British side, fought like a very demon. With his own hand he killed or wounded several Frenchmen, including an officer. Throwing away his sword he seized a musket from a soldier's hands and continued to fight until a grenadier had run a bayonet clear down his throat, and driven the point of it out at the side of his neck. A French chasseur, on the other hand, received a ball in his right arm. Grasping his sword with his left, he went on fighting desperately. Presently a ball entered his left breast ; but, still undaunted, he remained on the spot, slashing at the enemy with might and main. In the end a royal soldier pierced him with a bayonet, and the brave Frenchman fell to the earth a corpse.[1]

Captain of Grenadiers Laugerat was struck by a shell which shattered his shoulder. Raising him-

[1] *Jones' Narrative of the Insurrection.*

7

self as well as he could, he continued to encourage his men. "Friends," he cried, "do not trouble yourselves about me. Go forward to victory; she awaits you. Let me remain here, for I die happy." These were his last words. A grenadier of the same detachment, being mortally wounded, turned to one of his comrades with the words: "Take these cartridges; send them to those rascals." Then grasping his gun in a feverish embrace, he exclaimed, "Thus dies a French grenadier!" Even in the last agonies of death the man's love of display had not deserted him.[1]

While the better men of the British forces were spilling their blood in defence of the flag and their country's honor, their comrades were speeding over the highroad to Holly-mount and Tuam. Lake, accompanied by his staff, rode furiously along in the midst of the fugitives, with livid face and compressed lips. He cast not a glance behind him, nor heeded the surrounding turmoil. His haughty and aggressive spirit was smarting under the humiliation of defeat, for which he knew that he alone was to blame. Hutchinson felt the pangs of mortification no less than his commander, but to him this was not a time for vain regrets. He directed all his efforts to rallying the men and turning the flight into the semblance of an orderly retreat. He was not successful. Neither persuasion, commands nor threats availed to stem their wild stampede.

[1] Fontaine's *Notice Historique*, page 20.

LAKE'S FLIGHT FROM CASTLEBAR.

On they rode, hearing a menace in every whisper of the wind, a cannonade in every rustling of the leaves. Beside this, John Gilpin's famous pace sinks to the level of a peddler's jog, nor did Tam O'Shanter's Mag e'er display such mettle as their panting, sweating beasts, spurred on until the blood dripped from their flanks. So great was their fright, indeed, that they never stopped for breath until they had reached the town of Tuam, forty miles away; and even here they paused scarce long enough to eat, and then made on to Athlone. At this place an officer of carabineers, with sixty of his men, arrived on the afternoon of the 29th of September. These heroes had covered a distance of over seventy English miles in twenty-seven hours! No wonder the battle has been jocularly styled "the races of Castlebar"!

CHAPTER VI.

THE flight of the British from Castlebar was marked by an episode of which two distinct and widely different versions have been handed down by contemporaneous writers. According to British official accounts, a party of French dragoons pursued the retreating army above a mile from the town and took a piece of cannon, which they were on the point of turning on their rear, but a party of Lord Roden's Fencibles rescued the gun and killed five of them.

The other side of the story is as follows: It appears that when Humbert entered Castlebar and witnessed the utter demoralization of the enemy he instructed Bartholomew Teeling to secure the swiftest horses in the town for himself and an escort, and follow up General Lake with proposals for a capitulation of the British army. Teeling had greatly distinguished himself during the day. He had been in the thickest of the fight, and single-handed had captured an English regimental standard. Wishing to pay a signal compliment to his subordinate, Humbert insisted that he should use the trophy as a flag of truce in lieu of the usual white bunting. As Teeling with his party crossed a small eminence in the rear of the retreating force, they were suddenly set upon by a body of horsemen, who, disregarding the flag of truce—probably not comprehending it—cut down every man but Teeling himself. They spared the latter only on account of his officer's uniform, but they took him along with them a prisoner. Forced to accompany the army in its retreat for many a weary mile, denied access to General Lake, insulted and threatened with death, Teeling preserved his dignity and stubbornly refused to communicate the purport of his message to the various officers who questioned him. Therefore no alternative being left to his captors, he was at length taken into Lake's presence. The commander-in-chief became furious when Humbert's words were transmitted to him; and well he might, for this was, as he considered, heaping insult on injury. Lake expressed indignation at the language of the message and indulged in personalities, whereupon Teeling protested in courteous but decided terms. This only increased the Englishman's rage. "You, sir, are an Irishman," he cried. "I shall treat you as a rebel. Why have you been selected by General Humbert on this occasion?" "To convey to you, sir," was the reply, "his proposal in a language which he presumes you understand. As to your menace, you cannot be ignorant that you have left with us many British officers, prisoners at Castlebar."

Here the interview ended and Lake sullenly turned away. Not long after General Hutchinson rode up and apologized with every evidence of sincerity for the rash act of his cavalry. He also brought an apology from General Lake—who had apparently reconsidered matters—coupled with the request that the French commander desist from reprisals. Teeling was given full permission to return to Castlebar, and an escort was placed at his disposal. He declined the escort, but insisted on a surrender of his flag of truce—a demand that caused some hesitation on Hutchinson's part, yet was complied with in the end. Accompanied by that officer to the limits of the British lines, Teeling set out for Castlebar. He arrived there early in the evening, anxiously awaited by Humbert, whose apprehensions for his safety had increased with his prolonged absence. A man of violent temper when aroused, Humbert swore dire vengeance on the murderers of Teeling's unfortunate companions, and it required all the Irishman's persuasive powers to calm his wrath and bring him to a more reasonable view of the matter.[1]

The battle of Castlebar cost the British dear. It is true that the official report places the casualties at " one sergeant and fifty-two rank and file killed ; two lieutenants, three sergeants, and twenty-nine rank and file wounded ; two majors, three captains, six lieutenants, three ensigns, two staff, ten sergeants, two drummers, and two hundred and fifty-one rank and file missing—also nine field pieces." But the testimony of many participants goes to prove that these figures underestimate the loss. Humbert, in his report to the French Directory, puts the enemy's casualties at " 1,800 men—of which 600 were killed or wounded and 1,200 prisoners —ten pieces of cannon, five stand of colors, 1,200 fire-locks, and almost all the baggage." Here again there is a palpable misstatement, although an excusable one under the circumstances. In order to keep up the interest at home in the progress of the expedition, and to secure the much-needed reënforcements and supplies, the French general felt justified in resorting to such exaggerations. In point of fact the defeat cost the English about 600 men, killed, wounded and prisoners, and the greater part of their artillery and stores. But this loss is trifling when compared to the humiliation brought upon England's pride. Some of her most decisive victories in the past had been won by forces numeri-

---

[1] C. H. Teeling's *Personal Narrative*, etc., pages 217–220.

cally but little larger than the one engaged at Castlebar;[1] and that this well-equipped body of men,
inured to hardship and military life by several
months of warfare, should succumb to a most insignificant foe, was the bitterest pill the nation had
had to swallow for many a day. For a moment it
seemed as if even the great Marlborough's achievements had been put in the shade; for, asked the
pessimist, had *he* ever beaten the French under
similar circumstances?

No absolutely reliable account has ever been
given of the French losses on this momentous occasion. Humbert, for reasons of his own, omitted
any mention of the subject in his report to his government. That they were very severe admits of
no doubt whatever. When, two weeks later, the
French army surrendered at Ballinamuck, it had
dwindled from 1,130 men—the number that origi-
nally landed at Killala—to 844. Of the 300 men,
more or less, who succumbed during the campaign,
probably two-thirds bit the dust at Castlebar; in
other words, twenty-five per cent. of the entire
French effective.[2] Among the dead were the chief
of staff, Grignon, and Lieutenant Moisson, who
charged through the town at the head of the

---

[1] Plassey and Quebec.

[2] Fontaine says: " This victory at Castlebar cost us forty dead,
and we also had a hundred and eighty wounded." But he does not
explain whether the losses of the Irish allies are included in this estimate. The probability is that they are not.

". . . "the officers in their shabby uniforms, ... the lithesome
Irish belles in their bucolic finery," . . .   —Page 105.

French cavalry. About a hundred of the prisoners were Roman Catholic yeoman from Louth and Kilkenny, who, when appealed to by Humbert's Irish allies, expressed a willingness to serve under the French flag. They were mustered in to a man.

Despite the hardships of their march to the field of victory, despite their decimation by shot and shell, the soldiers of the French Republic, once the conflict over, had thoughts but for distraction and pleasure. The Gallic nature, with its fantastic mobility, its violent contrasts, once more asserted itself. On the very evening of the battle, with the dead lying unburied on every side, with the unhoused wounded torturing the air with their moans, Humbert's officers brushed off the dust and powder of the fray and assembled all that remained of youth and beauty "to trip the light fantastic toe" from " eve till dewy morn." It was a strange scene —the large, bare hall, lighted by the mellow gleam of flickering candles; the officers in their shabby uniforms, some embellished with white bandages that would later blush with the blood of the wounds they concealed ; the lithesome Irish belles in their bucolic finery, whose simple minds were half repelled by these rough exteriors, half frightened at this reckless indifference to surrounding dangers and hardships, yet wholly fascinated by the martial halo that enveloped their "deliverers." The faint, wheezy notes of a spinet, accompanied by the screech of a fiddle manipulated by fingers more used to grasping a sword than a bow, supplied the music that wooed the too-willing feet to merry measures. Through the open casements the night air, still heavy with the breath of battle, entered to cool the hot cheeks of the damsels, and by its familiar odor to spur on the sons of Mars to softer conquests.[1]

Though Terpsichore elated them and Venus enchanted them, these heroes had still another source of gratification. The work of the morning had elevated them another step on the ladder of promotion. Sarrazin, already raised one grade at Killala, was now a general of division; Fontaine, who had led the cavalry with such decisive results, had become a general of brigade; and chiefs of battalion Ardouin, Azemare, and Dufour exchanged their rank for that of brigade commander. Every man, in fact, who had at all distinguished himself during the day—and there were few who had not—received his reward at nightfall.

During all that night bonfires blazed from every eminence around the town of Castlebar, and far out toward Westport and Newport to the west. By this the peasantry manifested their elation at the success of the invaders, and their readiness to take up arms for the cause. At Westport some depredations were committed on Protestant property, but the owners on fleeing to Castlebar found at least ample protection for their persons. By the morning

---

[1] Sir Jonah Barrington is the authority for this incident.

of the 28th the town was overflowing with peasants from all parts of the province of Connaught, some armed with rusty match-locks, some with pikes, and some with shillalahs. All were in a fever of excitement, and desired to be enrolled as soldiers of the Irish republic. Shouting their wild refrains, the throng marched through the streets in military order, their leaders bearing the "tree of liberty," surmounted by the Phrygian cap.

Although from the beginning Humbert had manfully opposed all attempts to despoil the loyalists of their property, it was beyond his power to prevent the pillage of the residences of Lords Lucan and Altamont. Taking advantage of the confusion occasioned by the capture of Castlebar, the insurgents ransacked these two magnificent mansions from attic to cellar. Lord Altamont's property suffered most. His horses and cattle were driven off, his wine casks emptied, and his handsome furniture smashed during the drunken revels of the pillagers. The carved doors were dragged from their hinges, and the stained-glass window panes shattered to atoms; in short, the work of demolition was complete. Of Lord Lucan it is fair to say that his treatment was undeserved. He had done much in the few preceding years to improve the town of Castlebar, which practically belonged to him, one of his recent improvements being the construction of a large linen hall, with assembly rooms.

This taste of the sweets of revenge, instead of ap-

peasing the half-intoxicated multitude, only served
to whet their appetites. After ravaging Lord
Lucan's house they proceeded to the Protestant
church, which they left an absolute wreck,[1] and
then assembled on a lawn to discuss the advisabil-
ity of a general massacre of the Protestants. The
French officers present protested vigorously against
any such course, and Teeling and O'Keon added the
weight of their influence to restrain the bloodthirsty
desires of the mob. A certain Dr. Crump, more
persistent than the rest, mustered a band of plunder-
ers and marched with them to Humbert's quarters,
where he formally demanded permission to indulge
in one hour's revenge on the Protestant population. He seemed to consider this a poor compen-
sation for over a hundred years of suffering at their
hands. His pious request was not granted. Humbert curtly informed him that any further aggres-
sion on loyalist civilians would be promptly pun-
ished. That ended all talk of massacre in Castlebar.

Several more houses were pillaged, however, one
being the handsome home of Lord Altamont's
brother, Mr. Dennis Browne, and another the residence of the Rev. Dr. Ellison, who has already
been spoken of as participating, while a guest of
Bishop Stock, in the defence of Killala. The reverend gentleman, after partly recovering from his
wound, was taken along by the French as a prisoner of war, together with about eighty other loy-

[1] *Jones' Narrative*, p. 296.

alists, including one of the bishop's sons. Unknown to Humbert, some members of the native contingent broke into the parsonage and carried off every article of value. This act greatly incensed the French general, who entertained a profound respect for his clerical prisoner. It is even said that Ellison's influence with Humbert prevented the levy of two thousand guineas on the town of Castlebar.

Taken all in all, the conduct of the French themselves during the occupation was deserving of all praise, and this eulogy applies no less to the individual soldier than to the chiefs. "Many of us," wrote a Protestant citizen of the town, "proved them both brave and generous; those who were lions in the street seemed like lambs in the parlor." But, as if fearful of having said too much in their favor, he hastens to add: "However, I have imagined this to be policy, and that if they had once conquered the country, they would in a mass cut off all who had opposed them."[1]

Another inhabitant of Castlebar has left an interesting account of the arrival at his house of a party of the invaders. He obtained their good will by supplying them with meat and wine. "The rebels," he writes, "who accompanied them at first, plundered us of various articles; but one day when they revisited us I alarmed my foreign visitors, who expelled and chastised them severely. One of

[1] *Jones' Narrative*, page 301.

them, by name Phillip Sheers, was from Holland; I
gave him my watch, but he kindly returned it;
another, Bartholomew Baillie, from Paris, was mild,
learned, and rather silent. He had been a priest,
but on the overthrow of his order became a soldier. He denied a future existence. One Ballis-
ceau, a Spaniard, was as intrepid as Hannibal.
Since the age of fifteen he had followed the profession of a soldier. He had been a prisoner in
Prussia, in Paris, and in London. He had been
confined in a dungeon at Constantinople. He had
crossed the Alps with Bonaparte, and fought under
him in Italy. His body, head and face were covered with wounds. He was a hard drinker, a great
swearer, and mocked religion; and yet he was very
fond of children, and never entered my apartments
without constantly enquiring for my wife, who was
on the point of lying-in. The fourth was from
Rochelle and the fifth from Toulon."[1]

It has been seen that, like all French commanders
of the day—men who had worked their way up
amid the turmoil and uncertainties of a revolutionary *régime*—Humbert had much of the politician
in his composition. He had graduated from a
school in which the soldier was taught to consider
the promulgation of republican doctrine as much a
part of his profession as the waging of war. To
this circumstance was due the initial mistake of
a campaign thus far crowned with the most unex-

[1] Musgrave's *Memoirs*, page 596.

ampled success. Instead of pushing forward after the enemy and making the best use of his victory, Humbert settled down to the task of forming a republican government for the province of Connaught. When his object became known purveyors of advice, candidates for office, pothouse orators and embryo politicians of every stripe and color came forward by the dozens. Every one of them wanted a voice in the councils of the new government ; every one had his own-little plan for the regeneration of Ireland. The very men who had studiously avoided facing the hated " Sassenachs " on the field of battle, were loudest in their claims for political recognition. It took Humbert a full day to rid himself of this rabble. But it cannot be said that any of his selections from among the natives were particularly happy. He was necessarily obliged to listen to all such as wielded influence with the populace, and the majority of these were demagogues or scheming clericals. One man whose counsel would seem to have carried some weight with the French general was Michael Gannon, a drunken priest who had formerly been confessor to the Duke of Crillon in France, and, after the latter's death, to his widow. At the commencement of the · great revolution Gannon, to escape persecution, returned to his home in Ireland. Like other Irish priests of the period, he affected to ignore the avowed atheism of the invaders. On one occasion he harangued a large body of insurgents from Humbert's window, in response to an urgent appeal to accept a military command. He told them in substance that he felt himself incapable of leading them in the field, but he would pray for the cause and fight by their side. He further promised to heal their wounds with holy oil, of which he held up a specimen in a bottle, amid the tumultuous enthusiasm of his audience. Gannon's usual attire consisted of a French military cocked hat and a suit of fine silk clothes, the property of his former master.[1]

On August 31st, or four days after the entrance of the French into Castlebar, a new civil government was proclaimed for Connaught. The governing body was to consist of twelve members, to be named by the French commander, with one John Moore as president. The town of Castlebar was made the seat of government. The first duty of the executive, as defined by the proclamation, was the organization and equipment of a force of militia and the furnishing of supplies to the French and their allies. The force to be created was to number eight regiments of infantry of 1,200 men each, and four regiments of cavalry of 600 men each. All persons having received arms or clothing and failing to join the army within twenty-four hours were declared "rebels and traitors." The closing paragraph of the proclamation required, "in the name of the Irish Republic," every male from

[1] Musgrave's *Memoirs*, page 601.

the age of sixteen to forty, inclusive, to " instantly repair to the French camp, in order to march in mass against the common enemy—the tyrants of Ireland—the English, whose destruction alone can insure the independence and welfare of Ancient Hibernia!"

The new republican government thus conjured into existence was but a mirage. The president—a weak-minded person, as the result showed—amused himself on the first day of his appointment, issuing assignats in the name of the French Government; and when the French departed, three days later, the whole legislative system collapsed. In the meanwhile the insurgents, after numerous quarrels among themselves over prospective spoils, also succeeded in electing a mayor for Castlebar, two high justices and six municipal officers. Half the zeal expended by them in this useless scramble might on the field of honor have turned the scale in their favor.

8

CHAPTER VII.

FTER organizing a govern-
ment for Connaught, Hum-
bert once more turned his
attention to the military situation, and began laying his
plans for a march into the
heart of the country.   In
a letter addressed to the
French Minister of Marine, three or
four days after the battle of Castlebar, he had outlined his programme in the following language: "As soon as the corps of United
Irishmen shall be clothed, I shall march against
the enemy in the direction of Roscommon (to the
southeast), where the partisans of the insurrection
are most zealous. As soon as the English army
shall have evacuated the province of Connaught, I
shall pass the Shannon and shall endeavor to make

a junction with the insurgents in the north. When this shall have been effected I shall be in a sufficient force to march to Dublin, and to fight a decisive action."

He explained in this letter that the slow progress of the French was due to the hesitancy of the Irish allies; and in order that "this handful of French" may not be obliged to yield to numbers, he asked that reënforcements be sent, consisting of one battalion of the 3d Half Brigade of Light Infantry, one of the 10th Half Brigade of the line, 150 of the 3d Regiment of Chasseurs à Cheval, and 100 men of the Light Artillery; also 15,000 fire-locks and 1,000,000 cartridges. "I will venture to assert," were his concluding words, "that in the course of a month after the arrival of this reënforcement, which I estimate at 2,000 men, Ireland will be free!"

Humbert was apparently ill-informed regarding the situation at the time he penned his appeal to the French Directory. The county of Roscommon was but a very small portion of the disaffected district, which in reality comprised counties Leitrim, Cavan, and Monaghan to the northeast, and Longford and Westmeath[1] to the east (see map). In

---

[1] Though revolutionary, the spirit of the insurgents was far from being republican, if the following proclamation, which was found posted on a church at Westmeath, may be taken as a sample of their ideas : "Take notice, heretic usurpers, that the brave slaves of this island will no longer lie in bondage; the die is cast, our de-

fact the revolutionary spirit extended even to Dublin. From the day of the French landing, the
village blacksmiths everywhere had been busily
employed manufacturing pikes, the "croppy's"
favorite weapon, and the preparations were now
complete for a general uprising and coöperation
with the French forces in their march to the capital.
It being generally assumed that the invaders would
select the shortest route, which was through Longford, it was determined to aid them by the seizure
of the town of Granard, a strong post situated on
an eminence near the county line. The leaders in
this movement were two men of property, Alexan-
der and Hans Denniston, who lived in the neighborhood of Granard, and although members of the
Mastrim yeomanry cavalry, had secretly espoused
the patriot cause. The advent of the French in
Mayo had been anticipated for months by the revolutionists in Belfast and many northern towns, and
when the news came of the advance on Ballina,
Hans Denniston repaired north to deliberate with
the rebel leaders. It was intended that the attack

liverers are come, and the royal brute who held the iron rod of
despotic tyranny is expiring ; nor shall *one* govern. Our holy old
religion shall be established in *this house*, and the earth shall no
longer be burthened with bloody heretics who, under the pretence of
rebellion (which they themselves have raised), mean to massacre us !"

> "The Fleur-de-lis and harp we will display
> While tyrant heretics shall mould to clay.
> Revenge! Revenge! Revenge!"

Musgrave's *Memoirs*, Appendix, page 165.

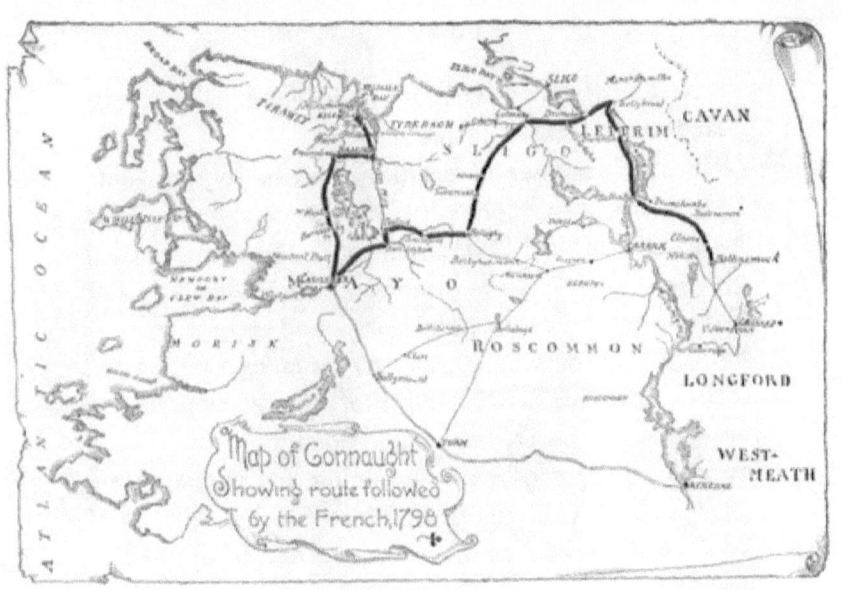

Map of Connaught Showing route followed by the French, 1798

on Granard, then weakly garrisoned, should take place immediately on his return.

In the meanwhile reënforcements to the Longford army came pouring in from all sides, Westmeath sending 3,000 men and Roscommon an almost equally large number. In Monaghan and Cavan, on the other hand, large bodies of men were held in readiness to march at a moment's notice and form a junction with their brethren as soon as Granard should be taken. The Monaghan army alone numbered 23,000 men, according to a reliable authority, and was armed with matchlocks, sabres and pikes, but lacked cannon and ammunition; and in order to make up for this deficiency the leaders proposed to attack the town of Cavan, containing a well-stocked depot of war material.[1]

As far as Humbert was therefore concerned, everything pointed toward a rapid advance in the direction of Granard. But here already the results of his dilatory policy commenced making themselves felt. On the morning of September 3d he was informed of the presence of Lord Cornwallis at Athlone, with a large body of regulars, and of the concentration of other hostile armies further south and east. He considered it inadvisable to encounter such a force with his insignificant body of French and his more numerous but entirely undisciplined Irish contingent; so, having learned from a spy named Jourdan that counties Sligo and Leitrim

[1] *Jones' Narrative,* pages 306, 307.

were comparatively free from the enemy, he decided
to adopt that circuitous route to the capital. He
sent orders to the troops he had left at Killala, and
a small detachment stationed at Ballina, to meet
him *en route*, and on the night of September 3d the
first division of his army, with the baggage and cannon, set out for Sligo. The next morning the second
division followed, about 400 Frenchmen and from
1,500 to 2,000 Irish auxiliaries. The majority of the
" patriots" had preferred remaining behind, presum-
ably to look after the "government."

On leaving Castlebar, the French general gave his
eighty prisoners their liberty, as they would only
have proved an incumbrance during the march.
Doctor Ellison was one of them. When the French
were fairly out of sight he sent a letter to Lord
Cornwallis, who was supposed to have reached Hollymount, fourteen miles to the south. Embold-
ened by the continued absence of the invaders—
it had been suspected at first that their departure
was but a feint—the Doctor by and by started out
himself on the Hollymount road, where he met
Colonel Crawford with a cavalry detachment, consisting of some Hompeschers—Hessian mercena-
ries—and Roxburgh Fencibles. Informed of the
state of affairs in Castlebar, the colonel proceeded
thither at full speed, accompanied by Ellison. They
reached their destination at a late hour in a pouring rain, and their appearance created a veritable panic among the insurgents. Crawford imme-

diately sent for John Moore, the previously mentioned "President of Connaught," and ordered him to disclose any information he might possess touching the route and plans of the French army. As the unfortunate man declared himself ignorant on the subject, the colonel ordered a dragoon to draw his sword and decapitate him. This bloodthirsty command so frightened the victim that he fell on his knees, invoked the saints, and begged for mercy, producing at the same time his commission as " President," an act of self-incrimination that can with difficulty be accounted for, unless, as has been stated by one writer, the President of the Province of Connaught was really under the influence of liquor at the time.

Let us now view the position of his Majesty's forces. On September 3d Lord Cornwallis arrived at Tuam from Athlone, with the army he had formed in the east, a portion of which consisted of the shattered remnants of General Lake's beaten forces. As the British commander lacked information regarding the intentions of the French, he resolved to continue his march to Castlebar with one portion of the army, while General Lake with 14,000 men [1] moved direct northward and joined General Taylor, who after the battle of Castlebar had retreated from Foxford and taken his stand at the village of Ballyhadireen. (See map.) Lake's division was made up as follows:

[1] *Jones' Narrative*, page 322.

the cavalry consisted of the 23d Light Dragoons, the 1st Fencible Light Dragoons, the Roxburgh Fencible Dragoons, and some mounted carabineers, under command of Colonel Sir Thomas Chapman, Lieutenant-Colonel Maxwell, the Earl of Roden and Captain Kerr; the infantry was made up of the Third Battalion of Light Infantry, the Armagh and part of the Kerry Militia, the Reay and Northampton Regiments, and the Prince of Wales' Fencible Regiment of Fusileers, under the orders of Lieutenant-Colonel Innes of the 64th Regiment, Lord Viscount Gosford, the Earl of Glandore, Major Ross, Lieutenant-Colonel Bulkeley and Lieutenant-Colonel McCartney.[1]

This army marched from Tuam on the afternoon of September the 4th, and late the same evening reached Ballinlough, about twenty miles to the north. Another day's march brought it to Ballyhadireen, where Taylor's brigade was encamped. At one o'clock of the 5th, Lieutenant-Colonel Meade was sent out by Lake, with a party of dragoons, to reconnoitre the surroundings and discover whether the rumors of Humbert's departure from Castlebar were true. At a hamlet between Ballyhadireen and Ballahy, an advanced patrol of the reconnoiterers captured a rebel, from whom they learned that the French were on the march northward. This information being communicated to General Lake, Meade was ordered to carry it to

[1] General Lake's Letter to Colonel Taylor, Sept. 8, 1798.

Lord Cornwallis at Hollymount. When within fifteen miles of Castlebar, Meade's dragoons fell in with a large detachment of insurgents, posted on a row of hillocks extending down to a bog. The foremost horsemen, without waiting for their superiors' orders, dashed at a party of pikemen stationed at a bridge, and very nearly brought on a general conflict, which would doubtless have proved disastrous to the colonel's mission. Meade, with great presence of mind, spurred to the front and ordered a halt, and perceiving that the rebels were acting in a half-hearted manner, offered them favorable conditions of surrender, which many accepted. The poor wretches had deserted from the French, and were suffering the pangs of hunger and the anguish of apprehension. About sixty muskets were surrendered to the English, after which the prisoners were allowed to depart in peace. Near Swineford, Meade turned to the south, and between Clare and Ballyhanis met the lord-lieutenant, who, having been informed while at Hollymount of the evacuation of Castlebar, was now on his way to the northeast to coöperate with General Lake's division in an advance on the French rear.

Rain fell in torrents when Humbert's army began its march, and the difficulties of the advance were increased tenfold by the muddy condition of the highways. Reports, unfortunately too true, of the hourly growth of the enemy's forces, served to act as a damper on the spirits of the Irish allies, and

those who had clamored loudest for the extinction
of their Protestant fellow-citizens now dropped out
by degrees from the marching ranks, and took
themselves off to a place of safety. The deser-
tions, in fact, became so frequent and general, that
a guard of French soldiers was finally placed on the
flanks and the rear of the Irish column, to check
them as far as possible.

The first halt of the army was at a place called
Barleyfield, the seat of a wealthy land-owner
named McManus. Here the French requisitioned
some provisions to be sent on to Swineford, which
place the army entered early on the evening of
the 4th. Humbert remained unremittingly in the
midst of his troops, not even leaving them to par-
take of his meals under cover of a farm-house.
From Swineford the army proceeded to Ballahy,
and after another short halt continued on to Tubbercurry. This village was the scene of the first
blood shed during the second half of Humbert's
campaign. The Corrailiney and Coolavin yeoman
cavalry, under Captain O'Hara, advanced to meet
the French at the outskirts of the place, and were
driven into flight after a short engagement. The
British lost one man killed, several wounded, and
two prisoners, Captain Russell and Lieutenant
Knott. At Tubbercurry the French were joined
by a considerable body of rebels who had marched
across the mountains from Ballina. They brought
with them some Protestant prisoners. These

COLONEL CHARLES VEREKER.

Humbert immediately sent back for the same reasons that had induced him to liberate their brethren at Castlebar.

The march was uninterrupted after this until the
army arrived, on the 5th, at Coloney, a romantic
village on the banks of the river of the same name,
ten miles to the south of the flourishing sea-port of
Sligo. The garrison of the latter place numbered
six hundred men of all arms, under Colonel Charles
Vereker, who, learning from O'Hara of the approach of the French, marched out against them
with two hundred and fifty of the Limerick City
Militia, twenty of the Essex Fencible Infantry,
thirty yeomen, a troop of the 24th Regiment of
Light Dragoons and two curricle guns. The inhabitants of Sligo, in the mean time, became a prey
to the greatest consternation, expecting to witness
scenes of rapine and plunder in their very midst ;
and their fears were not unjustified either, for the
town contained property valued at several hundred
thousand pounds, and its harbor was filled with
vessels of every size and description. In other
words, it offered many temptations to a hostile
force.

According to the colonel's own account, when he
arrived within sight of Coloney, at about half-past
two on the 5th, he found the French posted on the
northern side of the town ready to receive him.
His left was sufficiently protected by the river, and
in order to secure his right he sent Major Ormsby

with one hundred men to occupy a neighboring eminence.   The action that followed was obstinately contested. Vereker, with a boldness out of all proportion to his numerical strength, moved forward on the foe along the whole line, and for a while succeeded in maintaining himself. But the French reserves presently came up, and Humbert was enabled to outflank the British right and drive Ormsby and his men into the plain beyond.   Fresh bodies of troops were then thrown upon Vereker's right flanks with a view to surrounding him and forcing him to surrender, with the alternative of being driven into the water. The gallant Englishman, who had already received a painful wound, discovered the purpose of his adversary, and having expended nearly all his ammunition ordered a retreat. The British left the field in good order, covered by their cavalry under Captain Whistler, who experienced the satisfaction of repulsing a charge of the French Chasseurs. Notwithstanding the exertions of Captain Slessor, of the Royal Irish Artillery, the two guns had to be abandoned in consequence of the killing of one of the horses. However, as the ammunition wagon and entire gun harness were saved, the cannon proved of little use to the French. The casualties on the British side amounted to one officer killed and five officers and twenty-two rank and file wounded. The French loss was twenty killed and thirty wounded, and the rebels, who fought much better on this occasion than at Castlebar, also suffered to some extent.[1]

Humbert was not backward in paying a just tribute to the pluck and energy of Colonel Vereker.[2] He openly expressed his admiration of the masterly manner in which the British troops had been handled during the engagement, and declared the colonel to be the only man he had encountered in Ireland capable of leading fifty men into battle. The truth of the matter is that the French and British commanders at Colooney each miscalculated the strength of his opponent. Vereker imagined himself to be dealing merely with the advanced guard of the French army, while Humbert was led to believe that he had repulsed the van of a more formidable force. Expecting another attack the French general remained on the field for some hours, forming the rear columns for action as they came up, and then when no enemy appeared he turned to the east, following the high-road to Manor Hamilton, in the county of Leitrim.

Thus Sligo was saved from a hostile occupation, which was all the more unexpected as half an hour after the commencement of the fight at Colooney a number of fugitives entered the town, announcing that the English had been beaten and that the

---

[1] These figures are from Vereker's report. No French account of this engagement is in existence.

[2] Vereker afterward became Viscount Gort, and was permitted to adopt as his motto the word " Colooney."

French were advancing. The Protestant population was seized with a panic, and a stampede occurred to the harbor, where thousands of men, women and children boarded the ships in the hopes of at least saving their lives. A few hundreds of the younger men, however, secured matchlocks and pikes, with the determination of defending their homes at any cost, and their efforts were ably seconded by the Protestant clergy. The military who had been left behind by Colonel Vereker, under Colonel Sparrow, occupied the avenues leading to the town, and had the French appeared some desperate street fighting would have resulted. As it was, after an anxious night orderlies arrived from Colonel Vereker with the welcome intelligence that the French had abandoned their designs on Sligo, and the Protestants once more breathed freely.

General Lake, in compliance with the lord-lieutenant's instructions, was meanwhile pressing close on the rear of Humbert's army. From Ballyhadireen he marched on the afternoon of the 5th with his combined forces to Ballahy, through which place he learned the French had passed the preceding evening at about seven o'clock. He marched onward without further delay, and entered Tubbercurry at seven. He found Colonel Crawford awaiting him here with the Hompeschers and the Roxburgh Fencible Cavalry, and henceforth this detachment acted as the advance guard of the army. The services they rendered in harassing the French were invaluable, but their course was marked by the most revolting acts of barbarity. They took no prisoners under any circumstances, but cut down in cold blood all stragglers from Humbert's Irish contingent, and even entire bodies of the rebels who offered to surrender. Thus for miles and miles the road in the wake of the French army was strewn with the dead and dying, farm-houses and private dwellings in the vicinity were reduced to ashes, and devastation was spread all over a lately prosperous country. When the British force reached Colooney, whence Humbert had departed a short while before, a number of wounded French were discovered in a barn under the care of a surgeon. These experienced good treatment; but a Longford deserter who fell into the hands of the Hompeschers received short shrift, and his body, riddled with bullets, was marched over by the entire army.

To accelerate his movements the French general, after leaving Colooney, threw two pieces of cannon into a ditch and five more into the river at Dromahaire, a hamlet on the border of Leitrim. Crawford was close upon his rear, and shots were constantly being exchanged between pursuers and pursued. All this while the ranks of the Irish auxiliaries continued to thin out by desertion, superinduced by fear of summary vengeance; so that forty-eight hours after the evacuation of Castlebar scarcely half of their number remained with the army. The discipline of the French soldiers

under all these trying circumstances maintained itself in a most effectual manner. Neither lack of.
food and rest, nor the fading hope of ultimate
success could dampen their ardor. Their march
partook of the character of a running fight, devoid of one hour's respite from toil and danger,
and at times the enemy's cavalry would approach
near enough to occasion a hand-to-hand conflict, in
which, while invariably victorious, the French always sacrificed one or more of their meagre force.
Within a few miles of Manor Hamilton Humbert
learned of the concentration of rebel troops around
the town of Granard, and conceiving at last that his
only remaining hope lay in attaining this point,
whereby he would gain a strategical position of
great value between the royal army and Dublin, he
wheeled to the right and directed his steps toward
the south.

The same scenes that had marked his progress
from Colooney attended the latter portion of the
march. Crawford still hung obstinately on his rear,
and harassed him unceasingly with feints and partial attacks. Between Drumshambo and Ballyna-
more, however, the English officer overstepped the
bounds of caution and made a general attack, which
resulted disastrously for him, many of his men
being killed or wounded and the remainder put
to flight. Humbert was only prevented from surrounding the British on this occasion by the mistaken idea that he was engaged with Lake's entire

" Their march partook of the character of a running fight, devoid of one hour's respite from toil and danger."
—Page 128.

army. On the afternoon of the 7th the French passed the River Shannon at Ballintra, but so close was the pursuit that they were unable to destroy the bridge, as had been their intention. The powder used by Fontaine, who had charge of the operation, proved insufficient for the purpose, and only a slight break was made, which the British afterward repaired with the ruins of an adjacent house. At nightfall the French arrived at Cloone, and such was the exhausted condition of his men that Humbert found himself forced to give them a couple of hours' rest.

It was at Cloone that he received details of the progress of affairs in Longford and Westmeath. A delegation of insurgents from the neighborhood of Granard informed him that this post had been ineffectually assailed by 6,000 men on the morning of the 5th, and that the following day the patriot armies had experienced a similar check at Wilson's Hospital in Westmeath. Still, they declared that there was no reason to abandon hope, for though unsuccessful in their first efforts, the insurgents were in nowise discomfited, and, fully 10,000 strong, were feverishly awaiting the appearance of their allies, the French. The spokesman of this delegation is described by Fontaine as being armed from head to foot with a large variety of weapons, and bearing in a general way a not remote resemblance to the bold knights-errant of the thirteenth century. He appears to have been a very long-

9

winded and loquacious individual, for the same
writer attributes the fatal delay at Cloone solely
to these unnecessary *pourparlers*. From English
sources one learns of another cause for this loss of
time. It was the first opportunity the French had
had of closing their eyes in sleep during four long
days and nights. Every minute of that period had
been one of anxiety and toil. Humbert appears to
have given orders that he and his officers should
be awakened at the end of two hours, but the guard
let them sleep four, and thus the British army
came nearer than he expected. But for the loss of
that two hours the French might have succeeded in
reaching Granard, and then Cornwallis' plans would
have been upset.[1]

General Lake approached Cloone a little before
sunrise on September 8th. He had intended to
surprise the French during the night, but in the
darkness some of the divisions of his army missed
their route. The English entered Cloone on one
side as the French withdrew on the other.

Lord Cornwallis was on the high-road between
Hollymount and Carrick-on-Shannon, on the morning of the 7th, when an officer from Lake's division
informed him of Humbert's change of front. The
lord-lieutenant immediately guessed his adversary's intention, and while hastening his own march
to Carrick, directed Major-General Moore—who
had in the mean time been sent to Tubbercurry—

[1] *Jones' Narrative*, page 324.

to prepare himself for a possible movement against the town of Boyle.[1] Arriving at Carrick in the evening, Lord Cornwallis learned that the French had already passed the Shannon at Ballintra, and were bivouacked at Cloone. Accordingly at ten o'clock the same night he marched with his entire force to Mohill, ten miles further west, where at daybreak on the 8th he was confronted with the fact that Humbert was moving toward Granard. He thereupon sent instructions to Lake to attack the enemy's rear without delay, and himself proceeded with all possible expedition to St. Johnstown, through which place, on account of the breaking down of a bridge, the French would necessarily have to pass in order to reach their destination. (See map.)

In compliance with his instructions, General Lake, after reaching Cloone, redoubled his efforts to force Humbert to an engagement. He mounted five flank companies of militia, *viz.:* the Dublin, Armagh, Monaghan, Tipperary and Kerry, behind the Hompeschers and Roxburghs, and started them off against the worn-out foe. When the pursuers drew near, the infantry dismounted and kept up an incessant fire, and, aided by the cavalry, obliged the retreating troops to slacken their pace. Seeing that a battle was unavoidable, the French general finally brought his men to a standstill and made the necessary preparations. Defeat stared him in the face,

[1] See Cornwallis' letter to the Duke of Portland, September 9, 1798.

but, as on former occasions, he was resolved to up-
hold the honor of his country's flag at any sacrifice.
With his usual coolness in moments of danger, he
addressed a few words of encouragement to the
brave men who had stood by him through the long
period of trials and perils, and exhorted them to do
their duty to the very last. He posted the army on
a hill near the hamlet of Ballinamuck, four miles
from Cloone, and the same distance from Mohill.
His left was partly protected by a bog, and his
right by another bog and a lake. The position was
altogether as advantageous a one as could have been
selected under the circumstances, but the enormous
numerical superiority of the English reduced Humbert's chances, even of escape, to absolutely nothing.

At the very commencement of the action a most
regrettable incident occurred, for which no satisfactory explanation has ever been given. General Sar-
razih, who during the entire campaign had distinguished himself beyond all praise, was suddenly seen
to gallop down the first line of the rear division,
flourishing his cap on the point of his sword, as
a signal of surrender; whereupon the division
grounded their arms.[1]

At this moment the Earl of Roden and Colonel
Crawford advanced with their cavalry, and perceiving the movement in the French lines ordered the
trumpet to sound. It was answered on the French
side, and two British officers riding forward alone,

[1] C. H. Teeling's *Personal Narrative*, etc., page 227.

a parley ensued. The Englishmen demanded the immediate surrender of the French army. Sarrazin replied that the matter must be referred to the commander-in-chief, then stationed some distance behind on the Ballinamuck road with the main body.

While this conversation was in progress, General Taylor mistakenly informed General Lake that the French army had capitulated, and the British commander then despatched the "lieutenant-general of ordnance," Captain Packenham, and Major-General Craddock to receive Humbert's sword. The officers rode over to Humbert's line, but, to their consternation, were received with a volley which wounded Craddock in the shoulder.[1] Then it became clear that some misunderstanding had occurred. It appears that Humbert, upon learning of his subordinate's parley with the enemy, burst into a fit of indignation, and, repudiating any idea of surrender, ordered the advance at double-quick. Lord Roden had by this time induced Sarrazin to capitulate, and Crawford, confident of meeting no further opposition, had advanced on the French lines with a body of dragoons. In a moment all was changed. Humbert's Grenadiers rushed at the dragoons and

---

[1] An eye-witness of these events, whose letter appears in *Saunders' Newsletter*, Dublin, in September, 1798, declares that this volley was fired by a body of Irish rebels whom Craddock, in his kindness of heart, was urging to throw down their arms and flee, well knowing that no mercy would be shown to them by the vindictive Lake.

made them prisoners, together with their two leaders, while the rest of the horse, savagely attacked on
two sides, scampered away with precipitation.

Now the action became general. Lake, attempting to imitate Humbert's tactics at Colooney, threw
a column of troops on the right of the French, with
a view to outflanking them. Perceiving this Humbert withdrew his main body from the hill to
another eminence further back. The British artillery was then moved to the front; but when Lake
saw a large body of stalwart pikemen form into a
solid column for the purpose of charging the guns,
he ordered the latter withdrawn and continued the
battle with infantry and cavalry. On the brow of a
hill, a quarter of a mile from the spot where Sarrazin had surrendered, a number of French *tirail-
leurs* were posted with some artillery, and these did
much execution in the ranks of the British right.
The English general himself at one moment came
within range of their fire, and narrowly escaped with
his life. After a good deal of firing on both sides,
he at last ordered his light infantry and cavalry to
ascend the hill from two points, which they did
with enthusiasm; but not until every *tirailleur* had
either been killed, wounded or made prisoner, was
the French cannon finally silenced and the battle
won.

During the whole conflict Humbert maintained
his reputation as a skilful leader and a brave man.
Unwilling to survive defeat, he threw himself in the

midst of the enemy, sword in hand, and but for the intervention of his aide-de-camp, Teeling, he would probably have been killed by the dragoons, who bore him down from his saddle. Lord Roden and Colonel Crawford remained prisoners in the midst of a body of chasseurs until the Roxburgh Fencibles came up in search of their colonel. The French officers, realizing then that further resistance would only lead to the useless sacrifice of many valuable lives, surrendered their swords and ordered the firing to cease.

As far as the French were concerned the battle was ended. But now the most horrible act in the drama was to be played. The unfortunate rebels, who still numbered several hundreds, expecting no quarter, fought on with the frenzy of despair. Driven from the guns which they had helped to serve, not without loss to the foe, they fled into a bog and were here surrounded by horse, foot and artillery. Lake's hour of revenge had sounded, and he made full use of his opportunity. Raked with a galling cross-fire from all points, sabred by the horsemen and bayoneted by the infantry, there soon remained but a skeleton of the solid column that had stood side by side with Humbert's troops at the beginning of the battle ; and those who finally *were* allowed to lay down their arms only exchanged the bullet or sword for the rope. Here is what one eye-witness has written :

"We pursued the rebels through the bog—the

country was covered for miles around with their slain. We remained for a few days burying the dead—*hung General Blake and nine of the Longford militia;* we brought one hundred and thirteen prisoners to Carrick-on-Shannon, *nineteen of whom we executed in one day,* and left the remainder for others *to follow our example!*"

"They are hanging rebels here by twenties together," wrote an officer of the Reay Fencibles to his friends. "It is a melancholy sight, but necessary."

And here are another eye-witness' words: "There lay dead about five hundred; I went next day with many others to see them; how awful! to see that heathy mountain covered with dead bodies, resembling at a distance flocks of sheep—for numbers were naked and swelled with the weather. We found fifteen of the Longford militia among the slain."

General Richard Blake, referred to above, was a gentleman of Galway who had joined the patriot cause shortly before the battle of Castlebar, and had commanded a division of Irish auxiliaries during the later operations. His request to die by the bullet instead of the rope was denied. He bore his fate with the dignity of a hero, as did likewise one O'Dowd, another rebel of prominence. As the executions were proceeding on the battle-field, one of the doomed Longford militiamen demanded the reason for his condemnation. He was told that

"How awful to see that heathy mountain covered with dead bodies, resembling at a distance flocks of sheep."

—Page 136.

death was the punishment for desertion provided by
the military code. " Desertion indeed ! " was the
reply. " It seems to me the men who ran away
from Castlebar were the real deserters, and not I.
They took to their heels without attempting to
fight, and left me behind to be murdered by the
French." The force of the argument impressed itself on Lord Jocelin, who was standing by, and he
interceded with success for the man's life.[1]

Humbert was conducted before the English general immediately after his surrender. " Where is
your army ? " asked Lake, surprised at the small
number of his opponents. " There it is yonder,"
coolly replied Humbert, pointing to a group of
fagged-out men and horses in the background ;
" there you have my entire force." " And what did
you propose doing ? " asked Lake. Humbert seized
the opportunity to indulge in one of his favorite
fanfaronades : " I proposed marching on to Dublin," he answered, drawing himself up in a theatrical
attitude, " there to rend asunder the chains of those
who are suffering beneath your tyrannical yoke ! "
Lake shrugged his shoulders, with the remark :
" Such a project could only find birth in a Frenchman's brain." He thereupon ordered the French
general to be taken to the lord-lieutenant, at St.
Johnstown.[2]

The return of prisoners showed the French army

[1] Sir Jonah Barrington's *Rise and Fall of the Irish Nation.*
[2] Fontaine's *Notice Historique.*

to have been reduced to 96 officers and 746 men, with 100 horses and three field guns ; and of these survivors many were sick and wounded, or disabled by incessant marching. The brave men had marched almost a hundred English miles since the day of their departure from Castlebar. Their actual loss at Ballinamuck has never been definitely ascer- tained ; that of the British has officially been placed at three men killed, twelve wounded, and three missing, although there are reasons for believing that the figures were considerably higher.

The treatment of the French prisoners reflects credit on the British military authorities. They received many attentions and courtesies on all sides, and at Longford the officers were entertained at a sumptuous banquet. Expressing his surprise at the rejoicings and illuminations in the streets over the "victory," Adjutant-General Fontaine obtained the explanation, *sotto voce*, from an English officer, that his countrymen were really "illuminating their own stupidity and the triumphs of the French." The prisoners were sent to Dublin by the Grand Canal, and, as steam was unknown in those days, their journey lasted nearly a week. They travelled on six large barges, the first one carrying the escort of Fermanagh militia with a full military band, the second one the captive officers, and the remainder the rank and file. Nothing, according to contem- porary accounts, could exceed the nonchalance and merriment with which the French bore their situation. They seemed to consider that, having fully performed their duty as patriots and soldiers, they had every reason to congratulate themselves on the conclusion of a most trying and ungrateful task; so they were constantly collecting in parties, conversing with the utmost gayety, playing cards, dancing, and above all, singing the Marseillaise.

In Dublin—although, for prudential reasons, the prisoners were not allowed to show themselves in public—they were frequently complimented for their conduct during the campaign, and at their arrival in Liverpool an immense crowd gathered to greet them with many manifestations of friendliness. At Litchfield, where the officers were temporarily quartered, General Humbert was actually visited by a deputation of clergymen, headed by no less a person than the Lord Bishop, a brother of Cornwallis, who expressed their gratitude for the protection extended by him to the Protestants of Connaught.

Humbert's first request to the British authorities was that his Irish officers receive considerate treatment. He could offer no reason for leniency on behalf of those who had taken up arms against the Crown after the arrival of the invaders, but he insisted all the more on immunity for such as had come over from France and held commissions in the French army. Particularly solicitous was he about Teeling, his aide-de-camp. On this subject Teeling's brother has written feelingly, as follows: "After the surrender of the French army a cartel

was concluded for the exchange of prisoners, under
which General Humbert, with the residue of his
forces, was to proceed to France. The most bitter
regret was evinced by the French general in finding
that Teeling was not to derive the benefit of this
arrangement. The latter, as already observed, had
surrendered prisoner of war when his general was
captured. His person was easily identified ; recent
circumstances had made him known to General
Lake ; but (and I mention this circumstance with
a feeling of gratitude and admiration), though between him and several of the British officers on the
field an early and familiar intercourse had subsisted,
they had the generosity, under his present circumstances, not to make any recognition. On taking
muster of the French officers he was set apart and
claimed as a British subject by General Lake.
Humbert remonstrated ; he demanded his officer in
the name of the French Government ; he protested
against what he conceived a breach of national
honor and of the law of arms. ' I will not part with
him,' he exclaimed with violent emotion. ' An hour
ago, and ere this had occurred he should have perished in the midst of us with a rampart of French
bayonets around him ! I will accompany him to
prison or to death.' And this generous soldier did
accompany his aide-de-camp to Longford prison,
where he remained till the following day, when the
French prisoners were conveyed to the capital, and
thence embarked with the least possible delay on

board transports for England. Teeling was removed to Dublin to be tried by court-martial.
Matthew Tone, who had been arrested the day
after the battle, was also recognized as an Irishman
and retained for trial."

Teeling was brought to trial for high treason less
than two weeks after his capture, and, notwithstanding the many proofs adduced of his kindness
to loyal prisoners and his strict observance of the
rules of civilized warfare, he was condemned to
death as a traitor to his country. Humbert, on
board the *Van Tromp*, wrote a touching letter of
appeal to the president of the court-martial two
days before the commencement of the trial, from
which the following is extracted:

" Teeling, by his bravery and generous conduct,
has prevented in all the towns through which we
have passed the insurgents from proceeding to the
most criminal excesses. Write to Killala, to Ballina, to Castlebar; there does not live an inhabitant
who will not render him the greatest justice. This
officer is commissioned by my government; and all
these considerations, joined to his gallant conduct
toward your people, ought to impress much in his
favor. I flatter myself that the proceedings in your
court will be favorable to him, and that you will
treat him with the greatest indulgence."

Lord Cornwallis turned a deaf ear to all appeals
for clemency on the unfortunate man's behalf, and
on the morning of September 24th he was led out

from the *Prevost* to the gallows erected on Arbor Hill. He was attired in the full regimentals of a French staff-officer, and had attended to the details of his toilet with a minuteness bordering on foppery. He wore a large French cocked hat, with a gold loop and button and the tricolor cockade, a blue surtout-coat and blue pantaloons and half-boots. Around his neck was a white cravat, encircled by a black stock, very full and projecting, which the executioner presently removed in order to adjust the noose. The forty minutes that elapsed between the doomed man's arrival under the fatal beam and the completion of the hangman's task he passed in conversation with Brigade-Major Sandes, and until the very last no tremor was perceptible in his voice. Matthew Tone suffered death in a similar manner some days afterward.

The fate of these two men aroused a storm of indignation throughout France, where they were justly considered the victims of a breach of international right. Thomas Paine, the great freethinker, sent an appropriate protest to the Directory, recalling the case of General Lee, of the American army, whom the English were only deterred from hanging as a traitor by a threat of immediate retaliation.[1] The writer urged that the English officers captured at Ostend in the preceding month of May be held as hostages for the French officers of whatever ,

[1] See Appendix for the letter in full.

descent that had fallen into the hands of the enemy. He referred more particularly to the prisoners captured on October 12th of the same year,
when a French fleet, destined to renew Humbert's
attempt on Ireland, succumbed to a superior naval
force off Lough Swilly. The Directory, however,
in view of the disproportion between the numbers
of prisoners in the hands of France and England—
the balance being much in favor of the latter—felt
themselves powerless to act, and thus Theobald
Wolfe Tone, who accompanied the fourth expedition, fell a victim to the same relentless power that
had destroyed his brother.

CHAPTER VIII.

HILE effectually disposing of Humbert's "Army of Ireland," the surrender of Ballinamuck did not end the era of bloodshed in the unfortunate province of Connaught. Undismayed by the reverses of their would-be deliverers, the rebels scattered along the line of the River Moy from Killala to Foxford maintained their defiant attitude. More than that, barely three days after the surrender, 2,000 of them left Ballina under the leadership of Major O'Keon and Patrick Barrett, a former member of the local militia, for the purpose of retaking the town of Castlebar, which, as stated, had fallen into the hands of the British after Humbert's withdrawal.

In the early dawn of September 12th two citizens of the town, Edward Mayley and John Dudgeon, while stationed as pickets in the northern suburb, heard the thud of horses' hoofs approaching from the direction of the gap of Barnageehy, and presently descried two horsemen riding at a furious pace. The pickets sprang into the middle of the road and challenged the strangers with a " Who goes there ? " " A friend," said the foremost rider, drawing in his rein. " A friend to whom ? " " To the French," was the reply. " Oh, very well," returned the pickets; " where are you going ? " The strangers happened to be reconnoiterers of the advancing rebel army, and, ignorant peasants that they were, felt so jubilant at the distinction conferred upon them by their leaders that they gave free rein to their tongues. " We are going to take Castlebar," they explained; " we are captains, and there are 2,000 men following within half a mile of us." Scarcely had the words passed their lips when the pickets seized the bridles and, levelling their weapons at the riders' heads, ordered them to deliver up their arms under pain of instant death. The two rebels, who had evidently mistaken their adversaries for friends, surrendered on the spot and allowed themselves to be taken as prisoners into the town, where their captors raised an immediate alarm. This action doubtless saved Castlebar from recapture and probable pillage, for its defenders consisted only of a small body of

Fraser Fencibles, thirty-four armed townsmen, and a corps of yeomanry cavalry; an insufficient force at any time, but especially so when laboring under the disadvantages of a surprise.

Here again it were better to insert the words of one of the badly frightened citizens, some of whose reminiscences have already been quoted in a preceding chapter: "They (the pickets) entered the town shouting 'Murder! murder! Arise to arms, or you will be burned in your beds!' This echoed so loud, all the town rung with it; hundreds repeated it. Men, undressed, rushed into the streets; incessant rain heavily descended; the drums beat 'to arms! to arms!' whilst the dark, solitary walls reëchoed 'to arms! to arms!!!' At last the tempest silenced the drum; but no cause could allay the vigilance of our townsmen and the gallant handful of Frasers. The guards continued to bring in prisoners till morning. At last welcome day shone upon our afflicted town. To me it afforded much consolation, my wife being in the pangs of childbearing all night; though, I thought, will light save us? No; only serve to display our danger. Thus hope and apprehension bent alternately the balance. At length all our forebodings are confirmed by a discovery of the plodding assassins, planted to great advantage around the northwest part of our devoted town." [1]

It was fortunate for the Protestant population that

[1] *Jones' Narrative*, page 303.

their fate lay in the hands of so able and energetic
an officer as the commandant, Captain Urquhart.
At the very first note of alarm he assembled his
men in the market-place, and assigned them to
the most advantageous posts of defence. The main
body occupied the market cross, commanding the
principal avenues, with the only piece of cannon in
town; another division was posted between the
market-house and one of the city gates; and a
third, composed partly of cavalry, he stationed at
the north end, where the rebels were expected to
make their main attack. With a view to insuring
the safety of his small army in case of a retreat,
the captain placed a guard of infantry in a western street near the bridge, and a few cavalrymen at
the south entrance, on an eminence opposite the
church.

In this order the little army anxiously awaited
the expected attack, the issue of which, considering the enormous numerical superiority of the foe,
seemed scarcely doubtful. By seven o'clock the
rebels had concentrated their forces near the north
entrance and opened a heavy fire of musketry on
the devoted town. It was answered with much
spirit by the Highlanders. The latter, being under
cover, experienced little or no loss, while their opponents were picked off by the dozen. Seeing this,
Major O'Keon formed a column of assault and
made a dash forward, with the object of gaining
possession of the first line of defence. Smarting

under their losses, the rebels rushed furiously to
the attack.   Some were armed with matchlocks,
some with pikes, and the remainder with a variety
of weapons improvised for the occasion.   They
were received with equal bravery by the Highlanders and townsmen, who for the time being remained steadfastly within their defences, firing with
method and precision.   At last, at a critical moment, Mr. John Galagher, of the volunteer corps,
seized by a sudden impulse, broke from the ranks
and attacked the rebels at close quarters.   His
brother, the captain of the corps, did likewise, and
their example was immediately followed by the rest
of the defenders in that section.   So impetuous
was the charge that the rebel column scattered
before it like chaff and fled from the field in dire
panic, carrying with it O'Keon's reserves.   With
the exception of a small detachment under Lieutenant Denham, which remained behind to guard
the town, Urquhart now led his full force in pursuit of the fugitives.   Scores of these were cut
down by the cavalry or compelled to surrender,
and some who attempted to escape by way of the
Castlebar River and lake were engulfed in their
waters.

The complete defeat of O'Keon's army must be
regarded as a blessing, even by those who have the
Irish cause most at heart.   So inflamed were the
rebels by the exhortations of their fanatic spiritual
guides and their desire to avenge the massacres in

Wexford and Kildare, that the capture of Castlebar would inevitably have been accompanied by the
wholesale butchery of the loyalist inhabitants, and
that in spite of the restraining influence of O'Keon
and Barrett, both men of judgment and humanity.
In fact, one prisoner, with his neck torn by a ball
and two bullets in his body, confessed, between his
dying gasps, that it had been the intention of
many of his associates to plunder the town and
destroy every man, woman and child in it, including even the loyal Catholics! The feeling of relief
that pervaded all when they beheld the distant hills
swarming with the flying foe may therefore well be
conceived.

Before describing the closing act of the drama,
namely, the recapture of the last strongholds of
the rebellion along the River Moy, it will be necessary to dwell at some length upon the condition
of that section from the moment that Humbert's
march to the north left it virtually in rebel hands.
Thanks to Bishop Stock's admirable work, so often
referred to in these pages, authentic material is
plentiful on the subject. When the two hundred
French infantry withdrew from Killala, in the beginning of September, to reënforce the main army
at Castlebar, there remained in that town but two
officers, Lieutenant-Colonel Charost and Captain
Ponson; and they were joined later by Captain
Boudet, whom the advance of a loyal detachment
had forced from his station at Westport. To the

united efforts of these three heroes may be attrib-
uted the salvation of the Protestant population
from what, at moments, appeared to be inevitable
destruction.

Charost himself was a man of charming and sympathetic personality. To many he will appear an
even more interesting figure than Humbert. A
Parisian by birth, he settled in San Domingo early
in life, and subsequently married well; but the war
between France and England brought desolation to
him, as it had done to many others. He lost all his
property, and even his wife and only child, who
were captured while on their passage to France,
and taken to Jamaica. Unable to obtain any tidings
of them the poor man from sheer desperation enlisted in the French service, and worked his way up
to a lieutenant-colonelcy. Generous, humane, and
mild in manner, but notwithstanding this firm and
courageous in an emergency, he soon earned the
respect of Protestants and Catholics alike. In religious convictions he was practically a freethinker.
He told the bishop that " his father being a Catholic and his mother a Protestant, they had left him
the liberty of choosing for himself, and he had
never yet found time to make the inquiry, which,
however, he was sensible he ought to make, and
would make at some time, when Heaven should
grant him repose. In the interim he believed in
God, was inclined to think there must be a future
state, and was very sure that while he lived in this

world it was his duty to do all the good to his
fellow-creatures that he could." The well-inten-
tioned prelate appears to have attempted Charost's
conversion, but with indifferent success. He gives
him credit, however, for respecting the beliefs of
others, and taking scrupulous care, among other
things, that the divine services of the Protestants
at the castle at Killala should not be disturbed in
any manner whatever.

Ponson and Boudet, though each interesting in
his own way, lacked some of the sterling qualities
of their superior. The former was a curious little
body, not exceeding five feet six inches in height, of
most buoyant temperament. He was a Navarrese
by birth, "and," says the bishop, " his merry coun-
tenance recalled to mind the features of Henry of
Navarre, though without the air of benevolence
through them ; for this monkey seemed to have no
great feeling for anybody but himself. He was
hardy, and patient to admiration of labor and want
of rest. A continued watching of five days and
nights together, when the rebels were growing desperate for prey and mischief, did not appear to sink
his spirits in the smallest degree. He was ready at
the smallest notice to sally out on the marauders,
whom, if he caught them in the act, he belabored
without mercy and without a symptom of fear for
his own safety. He was strictly honest, and could
not bear the want of this quality in others ; so that
his patience was pretty well tried by his Irish allies,

for whom he could not find names sufficiently ex-
pressive of contempt."

In startling contrast to Ponson, Boudet, the later
acquisition to the French "garrison," is described as
being a man six feet two inches in height. "In
person, complexion and gravity," says the bishop,
"he was no inadequate representation of the Knight
of La Mancha, whose example he followed in a
recital of his own prowess and wonderful exploits,
delivered in measured language and an imposing
seriousness of aspect. His manner, however,
though distant was polite, and he seemed possessed
of more than common share of feeling, if a judgment might be formed from the energy with which
he declaimed on the miseries of wars and revolu-
tions. His integrity and courage appeared unquestionable. On the whole, when we became familiar-
ized to his failings, we saw reason every day to
respect his virtues."

Regarding Truc, the French officer left at Ballina, the bishop's verdict is not so favorable. He
denounces him as a man of evil disposition, lacking
both in common honesty and courage. Truc shared
his authority with O'Keon, and both stood under
the orders of Charost.

The first problem that presented itself to the
commandant after the departure of his men for
the front related to the means of maintaining the
security of the large district intrusted to him, em-
bracing as it did many square miles of rugged coun-

try, an extensive seaboard, and the towns of Killala
and Ballina. This whole section was swarming with
the armed bands of insurgents who had remained
behind for the purpose of plundering the Protestant
landholders in preference to joining the French in
the field. They numbered several thousands, and
might have constituted a sufficiently marked accession of strength to have changed the course of
events. In consequence of their turbulence and
lawlessness a strong guard at first nightly patrolled
the town of Killala and its suburbs; but as this
measure did not suffice to preserve the peace, Charost decided to offer the proper means of self-defence
to every well-disposed citizen. By a special proclamation the inhabitants of both persuasions were
invited to come to the castle and receive arms and
ammunition, with no other condition than the promise of restoring them on demand. The offer was
eagerly accepted by Protestants and Catholics alike,
but the result was a failure after all. From the very
first the insurgents protested against the arming of
their loyalist fellow-townsmen, their argument being
that the weapons would surely be turned against
themselves. The protestations soon turned into
menaces, which so intimidated some of the Protestants that they returned the arms on the very night
they had received them. The insurgents, not satisfied with this, adopted, on the few following days,
the tactics of harassing the loyalist minority with
domiciliary visits, ostensibly for the purpose of

searching for concealed weapons, so that from sheer desperation the unfortunates finally petitioned the commandant to call in by proclamation all the arms he had given out, excepting those in use by the recruits for the French service. With a lively appreciation of the situation Charost granted their request, and applied himself to devise another means for ending the depredations that were terrorizing the community.

In imitation of the methods employed by Humbert in the town of Castlebar, he issued a proclamation some days later, establishing a provisional government over the district within his care. He divided it into departments, each presided over by a magistrate, attended by an armed guard of sixteen or twenty men. None of these were required to declare themselves either for or against the king, being simply considered civil officers engaged in the service of keeping the peace. Mr. James Devitt, a substantial Roman Catholic tradesman of good sense and moderation, was unanimously elected civil magistrate for Killala, and thenceforth the town was regularly policed by three bodies of fifty men each, all standing directly under his orders.

However, as time wore on the task of restraining the evil passions of the ignorant multitude became truly herculean. Covetous eyes were cast at the bishop's residence, where, in addition to his family, the three French officers were housed. Few dwellings offered more temptations than his, for besides his own property it contained many valuables deposited in his keeping by the Protestant inhabitants during the first fright occasioned by the landing of the French. For the defence of the castle a guard about twenty strong was drawn from the garrison. The men were relieved once in twenty-four hours, but even they constituted a poor guarantee for the security of the household, imbued as they were with the idea that all Protestant possessions were rightfully theirs. At times the situation was most alarming, and only the tact and nerve of the commandant averted the threatened explosion.

On one occasion a drunken fellow named Toby Flannigan, who had promoted himself to the rank of major, arrested a Mr. Goodwin, a Protestant, for no other reason than that he was a Protestant. Word of the affair was brought to Charost while engaged in a game of piquet at the castle, and immediately the whole party repaired to the scene of the trouble. They found the " major" mounted on his charger, drunk and vociferous, surrounded by an admiring mob. Charost's order to release the prisoner was met by an impudent refusal. It was a critical moment. Failure to enforce his authority would have released anarchy and all its attendant horrors. Charost immediately ordered Flannigan to dismount. There was a ring of determination in his voice that brooked no delay. The culprit looked at his adherents for support, and finding none sullenly obeyed. Charost with his own hands divested him of his sword and pistols, and sent him under a guard of his own followers to the very jail that had opened its doors to the Protestant victim. This incident terminated Mr. Toby Flannigan's martial career.

Although the nominal head of almost all Mayo, Charost's personal influence extended, unfortunately, little beyond the immediate vicinity of Killala. At Ballina, thanks to the supineness or connivance of Truc, the insurgents were able to carry things with a high hand. Father Owen Cowley, of Castleconnor, was their leader. Being a master of the French tongue he had ingratiated himself in Truc's favor, and soon wielded almost unlimited authority over the town and its environs. His ulterior object seems to have been the extirpation of the heretics, and in pursuance thereof he steadily and deliberately labored to instil the poison of hatred and distrust into the Frenchman's mind. On the pretence of securing the young republic against the machinations of inside enemies, Cowley sent out bands of armed insurgents to arrest and bring to town the Protestant farmers of the neighborhood; and in a few days over sixty of these poor people, after seeing their houses demolished, were committed to a temporary jail in the house of Colonel Henry King. Having made sure of his prey, Cowley's next step was to gain permission to destroy them, but here he found an unexpected obstacle in the opposition of O'Keon and Barrett.

Suspecting the priest's designs Barrett interrogated him, and was haughtily told that Truc had given orders for the execution of the prisoners. Barrett flew to the chief, and through an interpreter laid the matter before him. It then transpired that Cowley had lied—a fact that Barrett took good care to charge him with in the most public manner. The young man's temerity, however, nearly cost him his life, for while he was still speaking one of the priest's followers made a lunge at him with a pike, and only his precipitate retreat saved him from the fury of the bloodthirsty mob.[1]

Cowley's methods and intentions savored strongly of the good old inquisition days. On the night of September 8th, about twelve o'clock, this disciple of Torquemada entered the improvised jail to gloat over his victims. They were packed together like sheep, in a room scarcely large enough to hold half their number. Surmising that in the confusion attending their arrest some Catholics might have been included, he greeted them with the words: "Lie down, Orange; rise up, Croppy." Robert Atkinson, of Ballybeg, one of the prisoners, noticed the speaker's clerical garb and approached him with a request for protection, but for answer received a stunning blow over the head with a heavy bludgeon. Cowley worked himself into a passion, and shaking his fist at the unfortunates, exclaimed: "You parcel of heretics have no more religion than

[1] Musgrave's *Memoirs*, page 629.

a parcel of pigs. I do not know whether you will
be put to death before ten o'clock to-morrow by
being burned with barrels of tar, or by pikes, or
by balls!"[1]   He supplemented this agreeable programme by adding his doubts whether balls "would
find room in their bodies." The priest's sanguinary
intentions were happily not carried into effect, for
when Charost's attention was called to the danger
of the Protestants he came in person to Ballina,
and reprimanded Truc severely for listening to any
accusations on the score of religion. He ordered
all persons arrested by Cowley's henchmen to be
brought before him, spent a full day in their examination, and discharged every one of them. The
poor wretches were free to return to their homes.
To many that word meant but a heap of ashes.

A volume, indeed, would not contain the list of
outrages committed in the name of Romanism and
—strange concomitant—Liberty! The malice of
the insurgents was early directed against a Presby-
terian meeting-house between Killala and Ballina.
It had been built for the worship of a small colony
of weavers brought from the north by the Earl of
Arran. Their pastor, the Reverend Mr. Marshall,
had devoted himself to fitting it up in a style
worthy of its character, and so universally was he
respected that all the Protestant gentry of the
neighborhood had contributed to its embellishment.

[1] Affidavits of William Stenson, John Armstrong and Robert
Atkinson. Musgrave's *Memoirs*, Appendix, page 164.

The building was utterly demolished in the beginning of September, and the congregation suffered much at the hands of the insurgents. Castlereagh, the seat of Arthur Knox, and Castle Lacken, the property of Sir John Palmer, were also pillaged by an organized band of marauders, and but for his indomitable pluck Mr. Bourke, of Summerhill, would have suffered in a like manner.

News of these various outrages having been brought to Killala, Charost despatched Boudet and Edwin Stock, one of the bishop's sons, to Summerhill to appease the mob, and another party of men to Castlereagh to save what remained of the provisions and liquors. The appearance of the emissaries ended the siege at Mr. Bourke's house; but the Castlereagh party, which consisted entirely of natives, could think of no better expedient for preserving the spirits from the thirsty bandits that coveted them than by concealing as much as they could in their own stomachs. The consequence was that they returned to Killala uproariously drunk. As for Castle Lacken, it was completely gutted, and the occupant and his large family were driven out to seek shelter as best they could find it. Charost's indignation at such barbarity knew no bounds. He told the insurgents that he was a *Chef de Brigade*, not a *Chef de Brigands*, and declared that if he ever caught them preparing to despoil and murder Protestants, he would side with the latter to the very last extremity.

In the meanwhile the suspense at Killala, with reference to the progress of the military operations in the east, had waxed acute. Contradictory rumors of an alarmist nature were constantly filling the air, and it was not until September 12th, the day of O'Keon's ill-fated attack on Castlebar, that some definite information reached the authorities at the castle. On the evening of that day William Charles Fortescue, nephew of Lord Clermont, was sent in a prisoner from Ballina, and from him Charost learned of the capitulation of Humbert's force at Ballinamuck. The commandant now felt that a crisis was approaching, for, aware of the temper of the insurgents, he had reason to fear that in the fury of their wrat and despair they would attempt the massacre of every Protestant in town. Conceiving his task of annoying the enemies of his country to be concluded for the present, he looked to nothing further than the preserving of peace and quiet round about him until the arrival of a regular British force should allow him and his companions to surrender without discredit. In pursuance of this determination, and with the distinct purpose to shed his own blood, if necessary, in the defence of the threatened loyalists, he took immediate steps to meet the requirements of the situation. In the apartments occupied by the three officers twelve loaded carbines were kept in readiness, and among the seven or eight trusted members of the bishop's household a variety of weapons were distributed.

THE BATTLE OF KILLALA.

Henceforth the Frenchmen remained constantly on the alert, watching not only all newcomers and applicants at the castle gate, but also their own guard of twenty men.

The precautions were by no means superfluous. Day by day the prospect grew more threatening. On September 18th intelligence of General Trench's preparations to march an army against them from Castlebar caused the insurgent leaders to send in a demand to Charost that the Protestants be imprisoned in the cathedral as hostages. This he flatly refused to do. The next day an angry crowd gathered about the castle gate, complaining that their friends and relations in Castlebar were being ill-treated by the British. To quiet them the bishop suggested that two emissaries be despatched to General Trench for the purpose of entreating him to do nothing to his prisoners of a nature to provoke reprisals on the Protestants at Killala. The proposition met with immediate approval. Roger Maguire, son of a Crossmalina brewer, and Dean Thompson, who with his family had occupied the bishop's apartments since the appearance of the French, were selected for the mission, and early on the following morning they started out on their perilous journey.

Their departure did not effect the desired truce. A false report that the English were approaching served to recall to town, on the 20th, a number of pikemen whom the commandant had induced, the

evening before, to return to their homes. Rioting
and drunkenness became the order of the day. For
the fourth or fifth time the house of Mr. Rutledge,
the customs officer, was attacked by a band of ruf-
fians in search of plunder. To restore quiet Ponson
was called from his couch, where he was sleep-
ing off the fatigues of the previous night. Single-
handed he rushed upon the crowd and felled the
foremost man to the ground with a blow from a
musket. The fury of his charge put the entire band
to flight. On the 21st another disorderly mob appeared at the castle gates and clamored for permission to arrest Mr. Bourke, of Summerhill, whose
defiant attitude had aroused their ire. They declared that he was abusing his Catholic neighbors.
Charost told them curtly to go to Summerhill if
they pleased, but added that he would follow them
up and fire upon them if he caught them in the act
of plundering the house. Later in the day the
commandant, by his presence of mind, averted another danger. Just as he was sitting down to din-
ner word was brought to him that a party of tur-
bulent pikemen had assembled outside the castle,
bent on plunder. Charost walked out leisurely,
accompanied by his two officers, and found them
preparing to batter in the gates. In his ordinary
tone of command he called "attention," divided
them into platoons, and proceeded to put them
through their daily exercise. His nonchalance
completely nonplussed them, and, occupied with

their drill, they were effectually diverted from mischief.

Much to the relief of the castle's inmates, the two emissaries returned the same evening from Castlebar. They brought a letter to the bishop from General Trench, giving full assurances regarding the treatment of the rebel prisoners. This was read to the insurgents, and appeared to reassure them. More consoling to the bishop was the information, privately imparted by Dean Thompson, that owing to the situation in Killala the general had decided to commence his march two days earlier than he had intended, and would probably reach them on Sunday morning, the 23d.

The preparations on the part of the British to suppress the insurrection in northwest Connaught had been considerably delayed by the ominous symptoms in the centre of the island. There, as has been shown in the foregoing chapter, an insurrectionary movement of great magnitude had been set on foot in the beginning of September, the intention of the rebels being to coöperate with Humbert's army on its march to Dublin. The surrender of Ballinamuck upset their plans, and none of the projected raids took place; but Lord Cornwallis deemed it imprudent to detach any troops from the main army until he had fully assured himself that all danger from a renewed outbreak was over. And thus it came to pass that fully ten days elapsed between the battle of Ballinamuck and General Trench's appearance in Castlebar with a force destined to restore the king's authority over the entire province.

Trench was determined that no loophole of escape should be left to the rebel forces. His plan was to attack them from different sides, leaving them no alternative but to surrender or be driven into the sea. Lord Portarlington, who was stationed at Sligo with the Queen's County Regiment, a small body of the 24th Light Dragoons, and several corps of yeomanry, was ordered to march to Ballina and form a junction there with the main body from Castlebar; and at the same time a force of 300 of the Armagh militia at Foxford, under Major Acheson, and another 300 men at Newport, under Colonel Fraser, were to converge to the same point from their respective stations.[1] Lord Portarlington's troops, being the farthest off from the common destination, were the first to move. Almost 1,000 strong, with two pieces of field artillery, they started from Sligo on the morning of September 21st. They were not molested until nightfall, when a body of rebels approached them at their halting-place, near the village of Grange. One cannon-shot sufficed to disperse the assailants. The British did not get off so easily on the following night. They had scarcely entered the village of Scarmore when they were attacked by a column of pikemen, who

[1] Extracts from General Trench's letters, dated Killala, Sept. 24th and 26th, 1798.—*Jones' Narrative*, page 285.

had advanced from Ballina under the command of O'Keon and Barrett. A prolonged and obstinate encounter followed, in which the insurgents were at length worsted. Before the commencement of the action, a number of Protestant farmers living in the neighboring hamlet of Carrowcarden had been impressed into service by the pikemen, and in order to insure their coöperation they were placed in the first line of battle. The natural consequence of this proceeding was their absolute annihilation by the royal troops.

The three remaining British divisions began their march on Saturday, September 22d. Major Acheson was vigorously assailed by a rebel command, but succeeded in beating them off. General Trench, whose army was composed of the Roxburgh light dragoons, the Devonshire, the Kerry and the Prince of Wales' Fencible Regiments, the Tyrawley cavalry and two curricle guns, took the road that had been made memorable by Humbert's advance to Castlebar. His progress was slow, for the rain, falling unceasingly, had converted the highways into beds of slime. The division entered Crossmalina Saturday night, worn out with the wearisome march. News of their approach reached Killala in the afternoon, and the pikemen at once demanded to be led against the foe; for with all their bigotry and ruffianism these uncouth peasants were never lacking in animal courage. Ferdy O'Donnell, of Erris, one of their leaders,

placed himself at their head, and the march began.
At Rappa the commander was taken sick and the
little army halted; but a reconnoitring party of
three mounted men, including Roger Maguire, already mentioned, pushed forward as far as the outskirts of Crossmalina. They there fell in with a
picket of sixteen cavalry, whom they boldly attacked and put to flight, actually following the fugitives into the town itself. The weakness of the reconnoitring party was concealed by the darkness,
and their appearance caused a veritable alarm—the
drums beating to arms and the soldiers rushing
wildly through the streets. Having attained the
object of the reconnoissance the riders departed at
full gallop to rejoin their comrades, whom they dis-
suaded from continuing the march, on the ground
that too little ammunition was on hand for a general engagement.

The march of General Trench's division was resumed at daybreak on the 23d, and in a couple of
hours it entered Ballina to find the town already
occupied by Lord Portarlington. Truc and O'Keon
had fled at the latter's approach, with the remnant
of their followers. No time was now lost in pushing the operations to a final issue. In order to cut
off all the avenues from Killala Trench divided his
forces, and while advancing with one division by
the common highway, he sent the Kerry regiment
of militia and some cavalry, under the orders of
Lieutenant-Colonel Crosby and Maurice Fitzgerald

(commonly known as the Knight of Kerry), to the same destination by a detour through the village of Rappa. It is a circumstance worthy of comment that, in spite of the difference in their routes, the two divisions reached Killala at about the same time.

Bishop Stock thus describes the engagement that followed : " The peaceful inhabitants of Killala were now to be spectators of a scene they had never expected to behold—a battle ; a sight which no person that has seen it once and possesses the feelings of a human creature would choose to witness a second time. A troop of fugitives from Ballina, women and children tumbling over one another to get into the castle, or into any house in the town where they might hope for a momentary shelter, continued, for a painful length of time, to give notice of the approach of an army. The rebels quitted their camp to occupy the rising ground close by the town, on the road to Ballina, posting themselves under the low stone walls on each side in such a manner as enabled them, with great advantage, to take aim at the king's troops. The two divisions of the royal army were supposed to make up about 1,200 men, and they had five pieces of cannon. The number of the rebels could not be ascertained. Many ran away before the engagement, while a very considerable number flocked into the town in the very heat of it, passing under the castle windows, in view of the French officers

on horseback, and running upon death with as little
appearance of reflection or concern as if they were
hastening to a show.   About 400 of these mis-
guided men fell in the battle and immediately after
it ; whence it may be conjectured that their entire
number scarcely exceeded 800 or 900.

"We kept our eyes on the rebels.   They levelled
their pieces, fired very deliberately from each side
on the advancing enemy ; yet (strange to tell) were
able only to kill one man, a corporal, and wound
one common soldier.   Their shot, in general, went
over the heads of their opponents.   A regiment of
Highlanders (Fraser's Fencibles) filed off to the
right and left to flank the fusileers behind the
hedges and walls; they had marshy ground on the
left to surmount before they could come upon their
object, which occasioned some delay, but at length
they reached them and made sad havoc among
them.   Then followed the Queen's County militia
and the Devonshire, which last regiment had a great
share in the honor of the day.   After a resistance
of about twenty minutes, the rebels began to fly in
all directions, and were pursued by the Roxburgh
Cavalry into the town in full cry.   This was not
agreeable to military practice, according to which
it is usual to commit the assault of a town to the
infantry ; but here the general wisely reversed the
mode, in order to prevent the rebels, by a rapid
pursuit, from taking shelter in the houses of townsfolk, a circumstance which was likely to provoke

indiscriminate slaughter and pillage. It happened that the measure was attended with the desired success. A great number were cut down in the streets, and of the remainder but a few were able to escape into the houses, being either pushed through the town till they fell in with the Kerry militia from Crossmalina, or obliged to take to the shore, where it winds round a promontory forming one of the horns of the Bay of Killala. And here, too, the fugitives were swept away by scores, a cannon being placed on the opposite side of the bay which did great execution.

"In spite of the exertions of the general and his officers, the town exhibited almost all the marks of a place taken by storm. Some houses were perforated like a riddle; most of them had their doors and windows destroyed, the trembling inhabitants scarcely escaping with life by lying prostrate on the floor. Nor was it till the close of the next day that our ears were relieved from the horrid sound of muskets discharged every minute at flying and powerless rebels. The plague of war so often visits the world that we are apt to listen to any description of it with the indifference of satiety; it is actual inspection only that shows the monster in its proper deformity.

"What heart can forget the impression it has received from the glance of a fellow-creature pleading for his life, with a crowd of bayonets at his breast? The eye of Demosthenes never emitted so penetrat-

ing a beam in his most enraptured flight of oratory.
Such a man was dragged before the bishop on the
day after the battle, while the hand of slaughter
was still in pursuit of the unresisting peasants
through the town.   In the agonies of terror the
prisoner thought to save his life by crying out 'that
he was known to the bishop.'   Alas! the bishop
knew him not ; neither did he look like a good man.
But the arms and the whole body of the person to
whom he flew for protection were over him immediately.   Memory suggested rapidly :

"'What a piece of workmanship is man ! the beauty of the
world, the paragon of animals !   And are you going to de-
face this admirable work ?'—*Hamlet.*

"As indeed they did.   For, though the soldiers
promised to let the unfortunate man remain in
custody till he should have a trial, yet, when they
found he was not known, they pulled him out of
the court-yard as soon as the bishop's back was
turned, and shot him at the gate."

This engagement, so graphically described, nearly
proved disastrous to the brave men whose advocacy
of the great principle of religious liberty had already
exposed them to so many perils.   In the indiscriminate slaughter which followed the battle, the royal
troops, elate with victory and inflamed by revenge,
showed small respect for persons.   Charost's escape
from death was almost miraculous.   After having
done his share in the defence of the rebel position,

he had returned to the castle and surrendered his sword to a British officer. As he turned to enter the hall he was shot at by a Highlander who had forced his way past the sentinel at the gate. The ball fortunately passed under Charost's arm and pierced the heavy oaken door. The English officer here interposed and tendered an apology for the soldier's act. It is needless to say that every courtesy was shown to the French prisoners after this, exception being made of O'Keon only, who, in spite of his rank in the French army and his claim to French citizenship, was some days later sent a prisoner to Castlebar to be tried for high treason. In response to Bishop Stock's appeal in his behalf, he was acquitted of the charge, but enjoined to leave the country on the shortest notice.

Two days after the battle the three French officers were ordered to Dublin, and one can readily believe the bishop's assertion that he parted with them "not without tears." The story of their honorable and courageous attitude during the long period of disorders having preceded them to the capital, they were received there with many marks of consideration, and they enjoyed the hospitality of no less a person than the lord primate himself. On the report of Bishop Stock the British Government offered to return them to the French authorities without exchange, but this act of courtesy was not accepted by Niou, the French commissary. These men, he declared, had merely followed their line of duty. They had done no more than what was expected of any French officer in a like situation. They were therefore not entitled to special favors.

The fate of the insurgents who escaped sword and bayonet was a far different one. A court-martial to try them began its sessions on Monday morning, the 24th of September, and early on Tuesday the first two victims were handed over to the executioner. These were an irresponsible drunkard named Bellew and one Richard Bourke, of Bellina. The authority of the Crown continued to be asserted in a ruthless manner for many weeks afterward, and even six months later fresh victims were found to swell the lengthy list. There has been no hesitation in pointing out in these pages the many acts of insurgent ruffianism prompted by religious intolerance and race and political hatred ; but it is only justice to add that ruffianism and rapacity constitute the worst charges that can be preferred against the unfortunate peasants engaged, after all, in a struggle with a galling despotism. In the words of Bishop Stock, "during the whole time of civil commotion not a drop of blood was shed by the Connaught rebels, except in the field of war." This circumstance should in all justice have carried some weight with the conquerors and have dictated a policy of mildness and conciliation, instead of one of blood and fire. Yet what could be expected of men who in the name of the king and the constitution had already, months before, turned the most flourishing parts of the land into a wilderness?

*   *   *   *   *   *

And thus ended General Humbert's glorious but abortive expedition, as insufficiently supported by the French Government as by the United Irishmen. Any further examination into the various causes that contributed to the maintenance of British misrule in the afflicted country would be superfluous here. The foregoing narration of fact speaks for itself, and fully answers the question. The careful reader can only deduce the inference that the principal cause lay in the Irish people themselves. The fate of the expedition became a foregone conclusion from the moment the rebels showed their colors. Their inability to separate the political from the religious idea made them the subservient tools of men whose one aim was to supplant the reigning despotism with a theocracy no less tyrannical. Had they been imbued with the same broad and liberal spirit which animated the thirteen colonies of America, their energies would not have been wasted in the waging of a petty religious persecution, but would have been expended in the field against the common enemy. What might not a force of 10,000 determined patriots, in conjunction with Humbert's army, have accomplished in the early part of the campaign? Probably an annihilation of Lake's forces. And

had the rebels done their duty even after the
French general's ill-advised sojourn at Castlebar, is
it not fair to assume that the result of the battle
of Ballinamuck would have been different? Even
though it may be maintained that Humbert's loss
of time at the village of Cloone practically sealed
the fate of the French army, and that at its best
his chance of ultimate success was problematical in
the extreme, it is certain that the onus of his failure rests primarily on the insurgents' shoulders.
Their cause was a noble one, but they failed to
grasp its true significance. May the lesson not be
lost on a future race of patriots!

CHAPTER IX.

Humbert's Career subsequent to his Return from Ireland—His Part in the Campaign against the Austrians, and the Expedition to San Domingo—His Love Intrigue with Pauline Bonaparte— Escape to America—Present at the Battle of New Orleans—Expedition to Mexico.

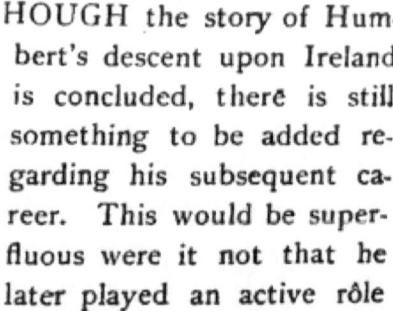

THOUGH the story of Humbert's descent upon Ireland is concluded, there is still something to be added regarding his subsequent career. This would be superfluous were it not that he later played an active rôle in the history of the New World, and that his name must ever be linked with the stirring events that created one of its great commonwealths. Fame he never acquired, but throughout this latter portion of his life he displayed qualities of no mean calibre. He proved himself a man of courage and ability, lacking but few of the essentials of greatness.

After his return to France, Humbert was de-

tailed to join Massèna's army, engaged in opposing
the Austrians in Switzerland and the Tyrol. The
situation there was critical for the French, who
were also menaced on their flanks by a host of
Russians, under Suvoroff. At the beginning of
June, 1799, the surroundings of Zurich became the
theatre of several obstinate engagements between
Massèna and the Austrian general, Hotze, and in
one of these Humbert received a severe wound.
He recovered, however, in time to take part in
the closing battles of the campaign, which terminated in September with the annihilation of Hotze's
army and the retreat of Suvoroff. We next hear
of him as a member of the expedition sent in December, 1802, by the First Consul, Napoleon Bonaparte, to San Domingo to crush the rebellion of
the black population of that island. It is notice-
able that our hero had received no further promotion in the mean time, and that the commander-in-
chief, Leclerc, who was Bonaparte's brother-in-law,
did not at first invest him with a separate command. This had its reason. Humbert had been
one of the opponents of the 18th Brumaire, the
coup d'état which practically ended the republican
era, and he had consequently incurred the displeas-
ure of the First Consul. Whatever his faults, he
can never be accused of lukewarmness in the cause
of liberty. He remained a consistent republican
throughout.

It is needless to go into the details of the horrible

Haytian war of independence, a blot on the history of civilization. As far as Humbert is concerned, he did his duty as a soldier with his usual uncompromising vigor. To him fell the task of dislodging the rebel general, Maurepas, from his position near Gonaives, while the other strategic points were being attacked by three separate divisions under Generals Desfourneux, Hardi and Rochambeau. Of these different corps, that commanded by Humbert was the most perilously placed, and its movements were impeded by heavy rainfalls. After some hard but indecisive fighting Humbert received reënforcements under General Desbelles, and the attack on the rebels was renewed. In the mean time General Leclerc sent another column against the rear of the rebel position, and finding himself almost encircled by the French, Maurepas at last surrendered to Humbert and Desbelles upon the condition, held out in General Leclerc's proclamation, that he should retain his rank.

The remaining divisions of the French Army were equally successful in their various undertakings, so that less than two months after the opening of the hostilities the rebel chiefs, from Toussaint l'Ouverture down, declared themselves willing to submit on honorable terms. An agreement was accordingly entered upon between the opposing armies, which might have eventually restored quiet to the island had it not been treacherously violated by the French commander. The arrest of Toussaint and

12

his transportation to France drove the blacks to
desperation, and the war was resumed with unparalleled barbarity. Decimated by the attacks of the
black guerillas and the ravages of fever, the French
forces dwindled down to the mere skeleton of an
army. The dreadful maladies generated by the
mephitic atmosphere, resulting from the decompo-
sition of the thousands of unburied' dead, spared
not even the commander-in-chief. On the night of
November 1st he died, after a prolonged sickness,
in the arms of his wife, the beautiful Pauline Bonaparte, eldest sister of the First Consul.

Pauline was a woman of fickle disposition. She
possessed, moreover, the passionate nature of her
race. Even during her husband's sickness her eyes
had rested favoringly upon the athletic and graceful
form of one of the generals of Leclerc's *entourage*,
and when it was decided that she should convey the
corpse back to France, she selected him as an escort. This object of her admiration was none other
than Humbert, and the world can scarcely blame
him for responding to advances from so distinguished a source. Indeed, Humbert seems to have
fallen fairly in love. When the couple reached
their destination he endeavored to secure the pro-
consul's consent to their marriage. Bonaparte, how
ever, had no desire for so democratic a brother-in-
law as Humbert, and fearing lest his veto might be
disregarded, he exiled the bold applicant to Brittany. Not satisfied with this, he afterward pre-

pared to throw him into prison—a fate Humbert avoided by making his way to the United States.

Little, if anything, is known of his movements during the first few years of his sojourn in this country. The war of 1812 found him actively engaged on the American side, and at the battle of New Orleans, January 8, 1815, he distinguished himself as the commander of a corps of Creole marksmen. One of the peculiar circumstances of the event was the coincidence of his finding himself on the occasion opposed to one of the very men who had contributed to his defeat at Ballinamuck. General Packenham, the English commander, had formerly been an officer in Lake's army, and had narrowly escaped death during that engagement in consequence of a premature announcement of the French surrender.[1]

The renewed taste of war's excitement seems to have fired Humbert's blood, and he looked around for fresh fields for his martial ambition. His glance needed not to wander far. The people of Mexico were in open rebellion against Spanish authority. From the frontiers of Texas to the extremity of Yucatan the spectre of war was pervading the land. Alternately victorious and defeated, the insurgents, first under Hidalgo and then under Don J. Morelos, had long defied the best troops of Calleja, the bloodthirsty Spanish viceroy. One of the incidents

[1] See page 133.

of the war was Don J. M. Toledo's abortive expedition for the relief of the struggling patriots. Toledo, who had been a member of the Cortes in Spain for Mexico, arrived in the United States at the close of the year 1812, and in conjunction with Don B. Guiterrez, then at Washington in the capacity of commissioner from the new Mexican Government, formed a plan for invading the eastern provinces of New Spain. They engaged some citizens of the United States to join the expedition, and set out for the *Provincias Interas*, and having entered the Spanish territories were reënforced by some guerillas. They obtained some advantages over the royalists, and took San Antonio de Bejar, the capital of the province of Texas. But they were attacked in January, 1813, and completely dispersed by Don N. Arredondy, military commander of the internal provinces, upon which Toledo made his escape to the United States.

At the time of the conclusion of peace between this country and England the situation in Mexico was anything but favorable to the cause of liberty. A patriot Congress convened at Chilpanzingo, ninety miles south of Mexico, had endeavored to revive the spirits of the people by offering them a democratic constitution; but in the end this body of representatives, by its lack of accord, only proved a hindrance to Morelos' operations in the field. When he or any of his generals proposed a military plan of action the long discussion which it must undergo in the Congress not only occasioned delay, but often defeated the object in view.

It was at this point that Humbert appeared on the scene. He had come in contact with Toledo in the city of New Orleans, and eager to join in any struggle on behalf of the oppressed, he set about to organize an expedition which should help the patriot army, then concentrated in Yucatan, out of the existing dilemmas. He succeeded in assembling over one thousand men of all nationalities and in chartering a vessel to convey them to the small port of El Puente del Rey, situated between Jalapa and Vera Cruz. In addition to this force the vessel carried a large quantity of arms and ammunition, then sorely needed by the insurgents.

As soon as Morelos learned of the arrival at its destination of Humbert's little army, he decided to join it with his available forces, and accompanied by the Congress. The march of the patriots commenced early in November, 1815, and although the royalists hovered around and harassed them continually, no general attack was attempted. Nevertheless, an unforeseen catastrophe prevented their junction with Humbert's hardy band. On November 5th, Morelos, the life and soul of the national cause, was surprised and captured at the village of Tepecuacilco while covering the retreat of his troops with a body of cavalry. The event cast a gloom over the Mexican ranks, not alone because the fate of their beloved leader was sealed, but because all felt he could not be replaced. Humbert vainly awaited the arrival of his allies in a country unknown to him and teeming with foes. He engaged the latter on several occasions, and with invariable success. He was also fortunate enough to receive reënforcements from the Rio del Norte and Nueva Santander. All that availed him nothing in the end. The utter disintegration of the patriot forces, and the advance of the loyalists toward the seacoast, soon placed him in imminent danger of being cut off from his only means of retreat. He therefore reluctantly concluded to return to the United States. The brave but unfortunate Morelos, on the other hand, suffered death some seven weeks after his capture. He was shot in the back as a traitor at the village of San Cristobal, eighteen miles from the capital.

Humbert took no further part in the sanguinary contest, which ended several years later with the establishment of Mexican independence. He died at New Orleans in February, 1823, passing the closing years of his life in comparative obscurity, and earning a modest competence as a teacher of French and fencing.

APPENDIX.

APPENDIX.

I.

THOMAS PAINE'S LETTER TO THE FRENCH DIRECTORY.

(From the *European Magazine*, November, 1798, page 353.)

CITIZENS, DIRECTORS :

The Irishmen who went with General Humbert, bearing your commission, have been taken and hanged. Those who have gone on the second naval expedition are exposed to the same fate. The following facts have a striking connection with the plan which I hasten to present to you.

General Lee, of the American Army, was taken prisoner by the English in 1776 ; they threatened to hang him. Congress, having no prisoners of the same rank, caused six lieutenant-colonels, prisoners, to be kept as hostages for him, and to be treated in every event in the same manner in which their general might be treated by the English. This conduct produced the desired effect. The general, instead of being hanged, was first set at liberty on his own parole, and afterward exchanged.

The Directory, among their prisoners of war in France, have many Irish officers who are attached to the British Government, and it is just that these Irish officers, bearing English commissions, should be kept as hostages for the Irish officers who have French commissions.

In another point of view, our descent ought to be assimilated to another descent, and the English officers taken at Ostend ought to be retained as hostages for the French officers taken in the descent upon Ireland. It is necessary likewise to observe that for more than a century the Irish have been used to go into the service of France, and to take French commissions, and that these commissions have always been respected by the British Government. The Irishmen who went with the expedition have in their favor a custom admitted and settled, and they serve under French generals. This differs greatly from the Emigrants at Quiberon. The Emigrants there were a separate body, acting solely under emigrant officers.

THOMAS PAINE.

II.

OFFICIAL RETURN OF THE FRENCH FORCES CAPTURED AT BALLINAMUCK.

General and other officers, 96 ; non-commissioned officers and soldiers, 746 ; horses, about 100. N. B.—96 rebels taken, three of them called general officers, by the name of Roach, Blake, and Teeling. The enemy in their retreat were compelled to abandon nine pieces of cannon, which they had taken in the former actions with his Majesty's forces.

Names of the principal officers of the French forces taken at the battle of Ballinamuck, September 8, 1798 :

Humbert, général en chef ; Sarrazin, général de division ; Fontaine, général de brigade ; Laserrure, chef de brigade, attaché à l'état major ; Dufour, ditto ; Aulty, chef de batallon ; Demanche, ditto ; Toussaint, ditto ; Babin, ditto ; Sibernon, ditto ; Menou, commissaire ordonnateur ; Brillier, commissaire de guerre ; Thibault, payeur; Puron, aide-de-camp ; Framaire, ditto ; Moreau, capitaine vaguemestre-général ; Ardouin, chef de brigade ; Servé, chef de batallon : Hais, ditto ; Mauchaud, ditto ; Brand and Massonet, officiers de santé.

Récapitulation : Sous-officiers, 96 ; grenadiers, 8 ; fusiliers, 440; carabiniers, 33 ; chasseurs, 60 ; canonniers, 41 ; officiers, 96. Total, 844.

P. ARDOUIN.

III.

GENERAL HUMBERT'S LETTER TO THE FRENCH MARINE MINISTER.

CITIZENS, DIRECTORS :   LICHFIELD, 2 Vendémiaire (*September* 25), 1798.

After having obtained the greatest success and made the arms of the French Republic to triumph during my stay in Ireland, I have at length been obliged to submit to a superior force of thirty thousand troops, commanded by Lord Cornwallis.

I am a prisoner of war upon my parole.

(Signed)   HUMBERT.

IV.

GENERAL HUMBERT'S LETTER TO THE BISHOP OF KILLALA.

DOVER, *Oct.* 16, 1798.

MY LORD :

Being on the point of returning to France, I think it my duty to testify to you the extraordinary esteem with which your conduct has always inspired me. Since I have had the good fortune of being acquainted with you, I have always regretted that the chance of war and my duty as a military officer have obliged me, in carrying the scourge of war into your neighborhood, to disturb the domestic happiness which you enjoyed, and of which you are in every respect worthy. Too happy am I if, in returning into my country, I can flatter myself that I have acquired any claim to your esteem. Independently of other reasons which I have for loving and esteeming you, the representations which citizen Charost gives me of all your good offices to him and his officers, as well before as after the reduction of Killala, will demand forever my esteem and gratitude.

I entreat you, my lord, to accept my declaration of it, and to impart it to your worthy family.

I am, with the highest esteem, my lord,

Your most humble servant,

HUMBERT.

INDEX.

FINIS

www.ingramcontent.com/pod-product-compliance
Lightning Source LLC
Chambersburg PA
CBHW030538040726
47497CB00008B/2507